THE PALATABLE PLATE
Cook Like an Artist
PARI DANIAN

*To your health,
Be delicious,
Much love,
Pari*

SCULPTRESS ART   DALLAS, TX

SCULPTRESS
ART™

www.SculptressArt.com

No Part of this book may be reproduced or transmitted in any form or by any means, electronic or mechanical, including photocopying, recording or by any information storage and retrieval system, without written permission from the author, except for the inclusion of brief quotations in a media review.

©2010 Pari Danian, All Rights Reserved

Book & cover design by goodmedia communications, llc
Photography by Pari Danian, Sculptress Art, LLC
Author photograph by Denise Keller

The text in this book is set in Palatino.
Manufactured in the United States of America.

ISBN 13: 978-0-9843444-1-3
ISBN 10: 0-9843444-1-1

DISCLAIMER: ALL INFORMATION MATERIAL FOUND HEREIN IS PROVIDED FOR GENERAL INFORMATION PURPOSES ONLY. THE INFORMATION AND MATERIAL PROVIDED IS NOT INTENDED TO DIAGNOSE OR TREAT ANY CONDITION OR SYMPTOM AND ITS USE IS NOT INTENDED TO BE A SUBSTITUTE FOR THE MEDICAL OR PROFESSIONAL ADVICE OR DIAGNOSIS OF A PHYSICIAN OR COUNSELOR. SCULPTRESS ART, LLC, DOES NOT WARRANT OR GUARANTEE THE QUALITY, RELIABILITY, TIMELINESS, ACCURACY OR COMPLETENESS OF ANY INFORMATION HEREIN AND THE INFORMATION IS PROVIDED WITHOUT WARRANTY, AND SCULPTRESS ART, LLC, SPECIFICALLY DISCLAIMS ALL WARRANTIES, EITHER EXPRESSED OR IMPLIED, STATUTORY OR OTHERWISE, INCLUDING BUT NOT LIMITED TO THE IMPLIED WARRANTIES OF MERCHANTABILITY, NON-INFRINGEMENT, AND FITNESS FOR PARTICULAR PURPOSE. SCULPTRESS ART, LLC, IS NOT RESPONSIBLE FOR ANY DIRECT, INDIRECT, SPECIAL, PUNITIVE, INCIDENTAL OR CONSEQUENTIAL DAMAGE OR ANY OTHER DAMAGES WHATSOEVER ARISING OUT OF OR IN CONNECTION WITH THE USE OF THE INFORMATION AND MATERIAL HEREIN OR IN RELIANCE ON SUCH INFORMATION OR MATERIAL, INCLUDING, WITHOUT LIMITATION, PERSONAL INJURY, WRONGFUL DEATH, OR ANY OTHER PERSONAL OR PECUNIARY LOSS, WHETHER THE ACTION IS BASED IN CONTRACT, TORT, INCLUDING NEGLIGENCE, OR OTHERWISE.

For Zahra

She fed many artists' souls.

In my kitchen's heart, there is always room for one more.

Recipe for a Loving Night

Ten beloved guests for dinner and
nine hours to prepare,

Eight herbs, tell tales of wisdom, from birth of a dandelion seed
to the growth of daisies in the field.
Mother Earth taught summer savory, sage, basil and chives
life lessons in one season and how to set apart from weed
Parsley, fenugreek and mint inspire to extend lives.

Seven spices beautify from inside out, with saffron in the center stage,
scented with nostalgic mountain air, got its color from the sun it praised.
Cumin, pepper and cinnamon defy age,
Angelica, turmeric and ginger carry the secrets to the flowers they raised.

Six senses engaged:
The sound of kettle whistles like my lover in the morning after,
The sight of rice dancing to simmering beats of a passionate sauce,
The touch of flour on my hands needing butter,
The aroma of rose water, awakens the fairies in the garden of dreams
The taste of salt and pepper, season the melting pot in harmony with each other
and,
the sense of humor that whips away onion tear, off my face.

Five fruits and vegetables, not just daily recommended,
Pomegranates and pears mentioned in the holy books,
Eggplants dress like monks, cabbage curbs rage
and jalapeño is not as devious as it looks.

Four courses to be served, one teases the tongue, one feeds the core,
the other reaches the heart and the last one soothes the soul.

Three candles for three wishes made and received.
Celebrate! Uncork the old bottle,
reveal the mysteries of a grapevine in every sip.

Two table spoons of zest from lemon and lime,
extend an olive branch
to the tossed salad in its prime.

One extra plate setting for a last minute surprise arrival,
my kitchen's heart is big enough for all,
"The more the merrier," we are all guests in god's dinning hall.

Zero left over and infinite love,
thank you angels and my beloved above.

Table of Contents

Preface .... pg 9
Cooking Tips & Notes
Pantry Arrangement
Spice Palette

Basics .... pg 18
Feta Cheese Palette
Basic Cooked Chicken and Broth
Basic Pot Roast and Beef
Basic Saffron Rice Palette (Polo)
Shirazi Salad Palette
Yogurt and Cucumber Salad Palette (Must-o-Khiyar)
Pomegranate Paste

Soups .... pg 34
Herb and Spinach Soup (Ash)
Lentil Soup (Adasi)
Meatball Soup (Abgousht-kufteh-Qelqeli)
Butternut Squash, Carrot and Barley Soup
White Bean Soup
Herbal Pomegranate Soup (Ash-e-Anar)
Cabbage Soup (Borsch)

Snacks & Lights .... pg 50
Eggplant and Mint Spread Palette (Kask-e-Badmjan)
Spinach and Yogurt Dip Palette (Borani)
Yellow Squash and Yogurt Palette (Yatim-Cha)
Eggplant Caviar Palette (Khaviar-e-Bademjan)
Red Bean Starter Palette (Lubia Mazeh)
Chicken Sandwich with Pineapple Palette
Parishki Palette

Salads .... pg 66
One-a-Day Salad Palette
Chicken and Potato Salad Palette (Salad Olvieh)
Shrimp Salad with Mango Palette
Romaine Lettuce Boat Palette
Butternut Squash with Pomegranate Palette
Romaine and Bean Potato Salad Palette

Light Entrées .... pg 80
Savory Meat Pie Palette
Cutlet Palette (Kotlet)
Herbal Meatballs Palette (Kufteh)
Chicken and Pine Nut Meatballs Palette
Stuffed Bell Peppers Palette (Dolmeh Phelphel)
Eve's Stuffed Apples Palette (Dolmeh Sib)
Stuffed Acorn Squash Palette
Skillet Kabob Palette
Mahi (Fish) Kabob Palette

Omelets and Egg Dishes ...... pg 100

Eggplant Omelet Palette
Date Omelet Palette
Tomato Basil Omelet Palette
Dill and Potato Omelet Palette
Asparagus Kukoo Palette
Potato Kukoo Palette
Grilled Eggplant and Tomato Omelet Palette (Mira Ghassemi)

Khoresh ...... pg 116

Gourmet of Filet, Parsley, Chives, Fenugreek Palette (Qorrmet Sabzi)
Gourmet of Fillet, Parsley, Mint and Celery Palette (Khoresh-e-Karafs)
Gourmet of Chicken and Eggplant Palette (Khoresh-e- Bademjan)
Gourmet Beef, Bell Pepper and Coconut Ginger Sauce Palette (Khoresh-e-Felfel)
Gourmet of Chicken with Walnuts and Pomegranate Sauce Palette (Khoresh-e-Fesenjoon)
Gourmet of Beef and Quince Palette (Khoresh-e-beh)
Gourmet of Fillet and Okra Palette (Khoresh-e-Bamieh)

Rice Dishes ...... pg 132

Chicken Kabob and Saffron Rice Palette
Lentil Rice with Raisins and Date Palette (Adas Polo)
Shish Kabob and Saffron Rice Palette
Spring Herbal Rice Palette (Sabzi Polo)
Saffron Rice with Lentil, Caramelized Onions, Raisins and Date Palette (Adas Polo)
Saffron Rice with Barberries Palette (Zereshk Polo)
Rice with Lima Beans and Dill Palette (Baqala Polo)
Rice with Green Beans and Tomato Rice Palette (Lubia Polo)
Rice with Carrots and Raisins Palette (Havij Polo)
Saffron Rice with Spinach, Caramelized Onion and Prune Palette (Esfenaj Polo)
Rice and Sour Cherries Palette (Albaloo Polo)
Rice with Meatballs and Cabbage Palette (Kalam Polo)

Sweetness ...... pg 156

Wish Palette (Rice and Saffron Pudding)
Receive Palette (Chocolate Raspberry Halva)
Celebrate Palette (Rice, Milk and Cardamom Pudding)
Rose Cream Puffs Palette (Naan Khamei)
Baklava Palette
Max's Ginger Bread Palette

Drinks ...... pg 170

BFF Cocktail - Bloody Mary Fun Fest Cocktail
Sin-a-Man Apple Martini
Angels in Oasis

Acknowledgments ...... pg 175

Preface

I come from a family of proficient cooks and restaurant owners. Though my sisters and my brother (chef and owner of Chez Max) were my muses in pursuing the culinary art, my mother was a domestic goddess who gifted me with her cooking abilities.

I learned even more about cooking after I married my husband. Although he never cooked, he taught me by eating my food and tasting the fruits of my labor. For years, each time he finished eating a meal I prepared he would comment, "Thank you, that was the best dish I have ever had in my life." This made me want to cook him finger-licking, delicious food every day.

Every time I was cooking something for the first or second time, I called my mother and asked her for instructions on certain traditional Persian dishes. She sometimes would offer to come and show me her ways and would share her secrets with me. In her younger days, she cooked for fifty people with only a couple of days notice. It was said about my mother that even her boiled water tasted like a piece of heaven.

My mother passed away a few years ago. Sometimes when I am cooking, stirring a saucepan or tasting the food, I hear her voice in my heart guiding me. Throughout the years, I have developed my own style of cooking, modifying the traditional recipes according to availability of the ingredients.

I created this book not only to share my personal and family recipes, all of which represent modern Persian cuisine, but also to share some secrets I picked up from a few of the amazing chefs I have met throughout my life's travels.

There is a saying, "Eat breakfast like a king, lunch like a prince and dinner like a pauper." I say, "Eat all three meals like an artist." Take your time to prepare for cooking, create the meal with the passion it deserves, and love what you eat. After all, we are what we eat, so be delicious!

Pari Danian

ARTIST PLATES ARE AVAILABLE AT EVERYDAYPARI.COM

Cooking Tips & Notes

The nutritional information on the spices and some of the ingredients were passed to me from my mother and family. My intention is not to cure any diseases. Please consult your doctor before starting any new dietary regiment.

Barberries, rose water, angelica powder, cardamom, pre-made pomegranate paste and quality saffron can all be found in any grocery store that offers whole foods and imported ingredients.

Create saffron solution by mixing one tablespoon of finely ground saffron and two tablespoons of hot water.

Liquid whey (kask) is drained and dried yogurt. It can be preserved in its dry form. It is remixed with water and used instead of cream in soups and dips. If this item is unavailable, use fresh yogurt or sour cream instead.

Use grape seed oil as a high-heat cooking oil, and use olive oil for salads and low-heat cooking. You may replace these two oils for any cooking oil of your choice.

All recipes serve four to six people

All stoves and ovens are not created equally, and neither are all saucepans. The first couple of times you prepare these meals, watch what you cook and note your stove and oven temperature variances, as well as the conductibility of temperature in your cooking utensils. All cooking temperatures are in Fahrenheit.

If you are going to use sugar, use a whole organic sugar in the raw. There will be no aftertaste in your mouth.

For salt, always use sea salt. You will know the difference after using it for while. All of a sudden you will become picky in restaurants and will say no to fast food without even trying!

If you cook it, your friends and family will eat it!

Pantry Arrangement

My mother always said, "Keeping sweet delicious spices in the pantry and the smell of good food invites angels to the heart of your home." I always make sure my home's heart is warm and happy by cooking daily and by keeping my pantry inventory well stocked and updated on a monthly basis.

Glass jars are best for locking in the flavors of the spices and ensuring all ingredients remain fresh. Glass also maintains the integrity of the spice's flavor. Do not keep a spice in a sealed plastic bag; if you have transported or have been given a spice in a plastic bag, move it to a glass jar for storing.

Do not keep chips, cookies, crackers and other packaged goods more than a week after they have been opened. The best thing to do is to buy them individually wrapped and fresh from the baker, or buy a small amount so there is not a lot left over.

Inventory your entire pantry once a month. As you clean the surface underneath all the containers, get rid of everything except for spices, salt, sugar, flour and canned foods. Spices are very powerful items and moving them around the pantry is great for the flow of energy in your kitchen—the heart of your home.

Contrary to popular belief, unless you are constantly cooking with other people, you can choose to leave everything in your pantry unlabeled. Preserve the mystery of your cooking by keeping your ingredients secret. If you forget what is in a jar or two, just open the jar and use your senses of smell and taste to refresh your memory.

Spice Palette

Saffron

The best saffron comes from north east of Iran. It is derived from the stigma of the saffron crocus flower. This miracle spice strengthens the stomach, can be used to soothe bronchitis and is full of beneficial minerals. Studies suggest that saffron induces happiness and is great for pregnant women as it assists with delivery. Saffron has many healthy benefits and should be a regular part of your diet.

Turmeric

Turmeric is a spice made of the root of the rhizomes, which is from the ginger family. This plant grows primarily in the Asian tropics. Turmeric's yellow color provides a beautiful color to many dishes. Meals prepared with this magical spice satiate hunger faster, making it an excellent spice for instant comfort food.

Cinnamon

Cinnamon is derived from the bark of several different types of trees in Asia. Like its color, cinnamon is a warm and friendly spice and goes with almost all foods and drinks. My mother taught me that if you can add salt or sugar to food, then you can add cinnamon to it too. Cinnamon has many benefits: it induces happiness and fights anxiety; it supports stomach and liver functions; and it can be used to treat insect bites and poison plant rashes. Cinnamon is also great for alleviating hiccups.

Sumac

Sumac grows in green clusters of small flowers on a shrub-like tree. It is from the cashew family, and the flowers bloom into tiny hairy fruits. Do not eat fresh sumac, as it is poisonous! Once it has been picked, washed and ground, it elicits a lemon flavor that is tangy to the tongue. Sumac can be used to sooth a toothache, and it strengthens the gums. Sumac is great for taking care of minor diarrhea and supports stomach function.

Ginger

Ginger comes from the underground stem of a plant primarily grown in Asia. It strengthens memory retention and supports the nervous system. Putting a dash of ginger in your soups helps relieve joint pains. This is a great spice for stomach issues.

Angelica Powder

Angelica powder is derived from the seeds of a plant mainly grown in Asia. Angelica powder prevents gas from building in the stomach and increases appetite. It cleanses the digestive system. Angelica powder is also a great spice to use for pickling or canning.

Hungry?

When you get to the crunchy part, stop eating … that's the plate.

Basics

Feta Cheese Palette

¼ pound feta cheese

small bunch grapes

pistachios

walnuts

cucumber

green onion

rosemary

mint

basil

radishes

dill

tarragon

cilantro

parsley

Use a few twigs of each herb. Arrange everything on an artist plate. Serve with toasted sesame bread or any other flat bread.

Spread cheese on a piece of bread, and place a little bit of herb on it. Wrap into a bite size and enjoy!

Be delicious!

Basic Cooked Chicken and Broth

1 whole skinless chicken cut in pieces
fresh squeezed juice from 1 large lemon
1 medium onion diced
½ cup water
sea salt and pepper
grape seed oil

In a medium saucepan, using medium-high heat, sauté the onion slightly till it wilts and glistens. Add chicken and brown with the onion. Season with sea salt and pepper and add lemon juice and water. Reduce the heat to low. Cover the pan, and let the chicken steam for 30 minutes. Pour broth in a bowl to serve with sprinkled chives or use in preparing various recipes.

Use the chicken in sandwiches or with various rice recipes. You may also enjoy the broth by itself. Chicken broth is good for treating colds and the flu.

Be delicious!

Basic Pot Roast and Beef Broth

2 pounds choice rump roast
fresh squeezed juice from 1 large lemon
8 cloves of garlic
1 medium onion diced
½ cup water
sea salt and pepper
grape seed oil

Whole lot of time!

Cut tiny holes in and around the meat, and place garlic clove in every slit. In a medium saucepan, using medium high heat, sauté the onion slightly till it wilts and glistens. Add meat and brown with the onion. Season with sea salt and pepper, and add lemon juice and water. Reduce the heat to low. Cover the pan, and let the meat steam for 2 ½ hours.

Pour broth in a bowl to serve with some sprinkled chives, or save to use for recipes that call for beef broth. The meat is used in various recipes with rice.

Be delicious!

Basic Saffron Rice Palette (Polo)

2 cups long grain white or brown Basmati rice
1 tablespoon sea salt
4 cups water
4 tablespoons grape seed oil or any other flavorless cooking oil
3 tablespoons butter (optional)
1 teaspoon saffron solution (See Cooking Tips & Notes)

Wash and drain the rice. Put the water and salt in a medium saucepan, and bring to a boil. Add rice. Stir once. Reduce the heat to medium-high so the saucepan does not boil over. After 5 minutes, the rice becomes longer in length and starts swimming in the simmering water. Before the rice gets sticky, drain the water by emptying the saucepan over a colander. Wash the saucepan and dry. Grease the bottom of the saucepan with a little butter, and add a little oil to it. Return the rice back to the saucepan. Melt a little butter and add the saffron solution to it. Pour in a circular form in the center of the rice, and spread it by gently fluffing the rice around the solution. Pour the rest of the oil all over the rice. Place a clean towel over the saucepan and firmly press the lid onto the saucepan, securing the towel. Steam for 20 minutes for white rice and 30 minutes for brown rice. Turn rice over on a serving platter.

If you use a nonstick saucepan, then the crust bottom (Tah-dig) will come out whole. Tah-dig goes great with the sauces of the recipes yet to come.

It took me a while, but I finally got the hang of making this rice. It takes practice.

Be delicious!

Salad Shirazi Palette

2 medium cucumbers

2 medium tomatoes

¼ cup dry mint

1 small onion diced

1 tablespoon brown rice vinegar

1 teaspoon sea salt and pepper

extra virgin olive oil

1 jalapeño pepper de-seeded and finely chopped (optional)

Wash and dry all the vegetables. Peel cucumber and finely dice in a bowl. Dice the tomatoes and add to the bowl. Add the onion, mint and jalapeño. Mix in brown rice vinegar and olive oil. It is best to prepare this an hour before the meal and refrigerate so all the flavors come alive. Transfer onto an artist plate and serve as a side dish or starter.

Note: lemon or lime juice can be used instead of vinegar if preferred.

Be delicious!

Yogurt and Cucumber Salad Palette (Must-o-Khiyar)

1 medium cucumber

2 cups yogurt

¼ cup raisins

¼ cup crushed walnuts

2 tablespoons dry mint or ¼ cup fresh mint

½ teaspoon cinnamon

1 tablespoon finely chopped onion (optional)

sea salt and pepper

Wash and dry the cucumbers. Finely chop the cucumbers, and put in a bowl. Add the rest of the ingredients. Mix well and season to taste. It is best to prepare this an hour before the meal and refrigerate so all the flavors come alive. Transfer onto an artist plate and enjoy as a side dish. If serving as a starter, serve with flat bread, bagel chips or sesame crackers.

Be delicious!

Pomegranate Paste (Robeh Anar)

6 cups pomegranate juice
1 tablespoon sea salt

Put the juice in a medium saucepan and bring to a boil. Stir in the salt and reduce heat to medium. Simmer, stirring occasionally until the solution thickens and turns to a syrup. Let cool.

Uses for Pomegranate Paste

Use the pomegranate paste for your drinks, salad dressing and sauces used in recipes in this book. Pomegranate paste is delicious in any recipe that calls for sweet and tangy flavor. For good health and weight maintenance, it is best to eat pomegranates or a spoon full of the paste a few minutes before breakfast. The sweet pomegranate paste is great as a cough syrup and soothing chest colds. It is also known to lift the mood. Fresh pomegranate juice is rich in vitamin B. My mother always gave it to me to strengthen my nerves. She said it strengthens decisiveness and gets rid of lingering and annoying doubts. Fresh pomegranate seeds are rich in iron and minerals, which can make them hard to digest. Add a little angelica powder to help with digestion.

In Persian countries, the pomegranate skin was used for dying textiles carpets and ceramics. This is a heavenly fruit. Get it, eat it and use it in your cooking!

NOTE: If using fresh pomegranate juice, you should be aware of two types of pomegranates. The sour ones and the sweet ones. If the juice is on the sweet side, add ½ tablespoon lemon juice to the paste. Save the unused portion in a sterilized bottle and refrigerate.

Be delicious!

Soups

Herb and Spinach Barley Soup (Ash)

3 cups largely cut spinach
2 cups finely chopped fresh parsley
2 cups finely chopped fresh cilantro
1 cup finely chopped fresh chives or the greens of green onions
1 cup chopped fresh mint leaves
¼ cup chopped fresh basil leaves
1 cup chopped fresh dill

¼ cup finely chopped fresh tarragon
2 medium onions diced
¼ cup brown rice
1 cup lentils
½ cup pinto beans
¼ cup garbanzo beans
1 cup barley

¼ cup apple cider vinegar
3 teaspoons turmeric
1 cup whey or yogurt
5 cloves garlic, minced
3 tablespoons dried mint
sea salt and pepper
grape seed oil

Wash garbanzo and pinto beans, and soak in water. In a large saucepan, sauté half of the diced onion with oil over high heat till golden brown. Add 2 teaspoons of the turmeric and stir. Remove the beans from water and add to the saucepan. Add barley. Add 6 cups of water, sea salt and pepper. Bring to a boil. Reduce the heat to medium-low. Cover and cook for 45 minutes. Wash and add lentils to the mix. Add all the fresh herbs and spinach. Add vinegar. Season to taste. Stir the saucepan with a large wooden spoon a few times. Bring to boil again. Reduce the heat to medium-low. Cover and cook for another 30 to 40 minutes, stirring occasionally.

In another skillet, sauté the other half of the onion and set aside. In the same skillet, heat one tablespoon of oil and put the garlic in the heated oil. Once the garlic is golden brown, add dried mint and the rest of turmeric. Stir once and remove from heat quickly. Put the soup in a small bowl, garnish with whey or yogurt, sautéed onions and the mint/garlic condiment.

Place on an artist plate, and serve with good friends and a whole lot of stories!

Be Delicious!

Lentil Soup (Adasi)

2 cups lentils
1 medium onion diced
fresh squeezed juice from 1 large lemon
4 cups water
1 teaspoon turmeric
1 tablespoon extra virgin olive oil
1 tablespoon chives
sea salt and pepper
grape seed oil

Wash the lentils. In a medium saucepan, sauté onion with grape seed oil over high heat till golden brown. Add the turmeric and stir once. Add lentils and water. Season with sea salt and pepper. Bring to a boil. Reduce the heat, cover and simmer for 1 hour stirring occasionally. Pour soup in a bowl to serve, and sprinkle with chives. Place bowl on top of an artist plate. Serve with a slice of toasted flat bread.

Be delicious!

Meatball Soup (Abgousht-Kufteh-Qelgeli)

1 pound ground beef

1 large onion diced

3 large tomatoes washed and peeled

2 large potatoes

½ cup pinto beans

½ cup garbanzo beans

½ cup yellow split peas

fresh squeezed juice from 2 limes

2 teaspoons turmeric

1 teaspoon cinnamon

1 tablespoon extra virgin olive oil

six cups water

1 tablespoon chives

sea salt and pepper

grape seed oil

Wash and peel the potatoes. Cut them into 2-inch pieces. Wash all the beans and the yellow split peas and place in a saucepan with the water and salt. Bring to a boil. Cover, reduce the heat, and let it cook for 45 minutes over medium-low heat.

In a bowl, knead the meat with 1 teaspoon turmeric, cinnamon, sea salt and pepper. Brown the onion in a large saucepan with some oil over high heat. Reduce heat. Make ½-inch meatballs from the kneaded meat, and put on the browned onion. Brown the meatballs with the onions. Add the rest of the turmeric. Stir to mix. Once the beans are cooked, add them with the water to the meat and onion. Add tomato, potato and lime juice. Let it simmer for 25 more minutes. Pour soup in a bowl to serve and sprinkle with chives. Place bowl on top of an artist plate. Serve with a slice of toasted flat bread and a side of Shirazi salad.

Be delicious!

Butternut Squash, Carrot and Barley Soup

1 cup butternut squash finely chopped in a food processor
1 cup carrots finely chopped
1 cup chopped celery
1 cup barley
1 large onion diced
½ teaspoon cumin seed
½ cup cilantro
½ teaspoon turmeric
3 cloves garlic minced

1 cup chicken broth
2 cups water
fresh squeezed juice from 1 lime
extra virgin olive oil
6 cups water
1 tablespoon chives
sea salt and pepper
grape seed oil

In a large saucepan, brown onion with one tablespoon grape seed oil over high heat. Add the turmeric and stir. Add butternut squash, celery, carrots, the cumin seed and a dash of salt. Stir and wait for the vegetables to glisten. Add the barley and water. Bring to a boil. Cover and reduce the heat, letting it simmer for 25 minutes. Stir in chicken broth, lime juice, olive oil and cilantro. Pour soup into a bowl to serve and sprinkle with chives. Place bowl on top of an artist plate. Serve with a piece of multi-grain artisan bread.

Be delicious!

White Bean Soup

1 cup dried white beans (or 2 cans of white beans drained)

1 cup carrots finely chopped

1 cup chopped celery

1 large onion diced

½ cup cilantro

3 cloves garlic minced

1 cup chicken broth

2 cups water

fresh squeezed juice from 1 lime

6 cups water

1 tablespoon toasted sesame

sea salt and pepper

grape seed oil

Wash and soak the beans. In a medium saucepan, brown onion with one tablespoon of grape seed oil over high heat. Add beans to the saucepan with two cups of water and a dash of salt. Bring to a boil, and then cover the saucepan. Let it simmer and cook for 30 minutes. (Note: If using canned beans, skip this step.) Add the celery, carrots, garlic, chicken broth and lime juice. Bring to a boil. Cover and reduce the heat, letting it simmer for 25 minutes. Pour soup into a bowl to serve and sprinkle with toasted sesame. Place bowl on an artist plate. Serve with a piece of multi-grain, artisan bread.

Be delicious!

Herbal Pomegranate Soup (Ash-e-Anar)

2 cups pomegranate juice
1 cup pomegranate seeds
1 cup yellow split peas
1 cup brown rice
2 cups finely chopped fresh parsley
2 cups finely chopped fresh cilantro
1 cup finely chopped fresh chives or the greens of green onions
1 cup chopped fresh mint leaves
2 medium onions diced
2 teaspoons turmeric

1 teaspoon cinnamon
2 teaspoons angelica powder, or 1 tablespoon angelica seeds (optional)
2 tablespoons brown sugar
3 cloves garlic minced
2 tablespoons dried mint
sea salt and pepper
grape seed oil
4 cups water

Wash rice and yellow split peas and soak in some water. In a large saucepan, sauté half of the diced onion with some oil over high heat till golden brown. Add 2 teaspoons of the turmeric and stir. Remove rice and peas from water and add to the saucepan. Add 4 cups of water, sea salt and pepper. Bring to a boil. Reduce the heat to medium-low. Cover and cook for 25 minutes. Mix pomegranate with sugar and cinnamon. Add all the fresh herbs, pomegranate sauce, pomegranate seeds and angelica powder. Season to taste. Stir the saucepan with a large, wooden spoon a few times. Bring to a boil again. Reduce the heat to medium-low. Cover for another 30 minutes, stirring occasionally.

In another skillet, sauté the other half of the onion and set aside. In the same skillet, heat one tablespoon of oil, and put the garlic in the heated oil. Once the garlic is golden brown, add dried mint to the remaining turmeric. Stir once and remove from heat quickly. Put the soup in a small bowl, garnish with mint/garlic condiment and the sautéed onions, and place on an artist plate.

Be delicious!

Cabbage Soup (Borsch)

1 medium white cabbage

1 pound beef for stew (preferably a meat cut with bone in)

1 cup pinto beans

1 cup carrots finely chopped

1 large tomato diced

1 large onion diced

3 cloves garlic minced

2 cups water

fresh squeezed juice from 2 limes

2 cups tomato juice

2 teaspoons turmeric

1 teaspoon cinnamon

sea salt and pepper

grape seed oil

1 tablespoon toasted sesame seed

Wash and soak the beans. Wash and cut the cabbage into ½-inch pieces. In a large skillet, heat 1 tablespoon oil and then put the cabbage in the skillet to sauté. Once the cabbage shrinks and glistens, add the carrots. Stir in 1 teaspoon of turmeric and a dash of salt and set aside. In a large saucepan, brown the onion with 1 tablespoon of grape seed oil over high heat. Add 1 teaspoon of turmeric and stir once. Add meat and beans with 2 cups of water and a dash of salt. Bring to a boil, cover the saucepan, and reduce the heat to medium-low. Let it simmer and cook for 30 minutes, or until the beans are soft. Add cabbage, carrot mixture, tomato juice, lime juice and cinnamon to the saucepan. Stir in all the ingredients. Bring to a boil. Season to taste. Reduce the heat to medium-low. Cover and continue to cook for another 25 minutes. Pour soup into a bowl to serve, and sprinkle with toasted sesame. Place the bowl on top of an artist plate. Serve with plain yogurt and a piece of rye artisan bread.

Be delicious!

Snacks & Lights

Eggplant and Mint Spread Palette (Kask-e-Badmjan)

2 medium eggplants

1 cup finely chopped fresh mint or ¼ cup dry mint

1 small onion diced

5 cloves of garlic

1 teaspoon turmeric

sea salt and pepper

¼ cup sour cream or whey

extra virgin olive oil

mint twig for garnish

Peel eggplant and cut into 2x3-inch pieces. Sprinkle salt on eggplant. Let it sit for 30 minutes. A brown juice will excrete from the eggplant. Wash the eggplant, and let it drain. Lightly grease a nonstick baking tray, and spread the eggplant on it. Spray or brush on olive oil (enough to prevent drying). Sprinkle a little sea salt on the eggplant, and let it bake in the center of a preheated oven at 400° for 30 minutes or until the surface of the eggplant is golden brown. While the eggplant cools, sauté the diced onion and 5 cloves of garlic (minced) in olive oil. When the mixture is golden brown, add mint, stir the mixture, then add turmeric and stir again. After 1 minute, remove from heat. Put the baked eggplant and the mint/onion mixture in a bowl. Use a masher to mix and smash the eggplant incorporating the mint/onion mixture. Mix in sour cream or whey. Transfer to an artist plate and garnish with a mint twig and bit of whey or sour cream. Serve with pita bread or sesame flat bread.

Be delicious!

Spinach and Yogurt Dip Palette (Borani)

½ pound organic baby spinach, or one small package of frozen spinach

½ small onion cut in thin slices

3 cloves of garlic

1 tablespoon lemon juice

1 teaspoon turmeric

½ fresh yogurt

sea salt and pepper

grape seed oil, or any other flavorless cooking oil

¼ cup crushed walnuts

1 slice of cooked beet for garnish

Wash and thoroughly drain spinach from excess water. In a big skillet using high heat, sauté onion and garlic together with the oil until golden brown. Add turmeric and stir once or twice. Immediately add the spinach to the skillet and stir to mix. Sprinkle lemon juice on spinach. Add salt and remove from heat once the spinach has wilted. Let the mixture cool in the refrigerator. Empty the excess juice around the spinach. Mix in yogurt, walnut and pepper. Add more salt if needed. Serve with pita chips, toasted bagel crackers or your favorite flat bread.

Be delicious!

Yellow Squash and Yogurt Palette (Yatim-Cha)

5 medium, organic, yellow squash
1 small onion cut in thin slices
5 cloves of garlic
1 tablespoon lemon juice
1 teaspoon turmeric
1 cup fresh yogurt
¼ cup water, chicken or vegetable broth
1 slice of beet and parsley for garnish
sea salt and pepper
grape seed oil or any other flavorless cooking oil

Wash the squash and cut the green top off. In a 6-inch saucepan using high heat, sauté onion and garlic together until golden brown. Add turmeric and stir once or twice. Immediately add the squash and stir to mix. Cover the top for 1 or 2 minutes to let steam build up inside the saucepan. Remove the cover, add the turmeric, sea salt and pepper and stir to mix the spices. Add the lemon juice and broth. Decrease the heat to low and allow to cook for twenty minutes. Remove from the heat.

Transfer to an artist plate, and garnish with a beet and parsley. Serve with pita chips, toasted bagel crackers or your favorite flat bread.

This dish may be served hot as lunch or dinner, or served cold as an appetizer.

Note: This recipe can also be used for a zucchini-yogurt dip. Just replace the yellow squash with zucchini.

Be delicious!

Eggplant Caviar Palette (Khaviar-e-Bademjan)

1 medium eggplant

1 large tomato diced

½ medium of each: red, yellow and green bell pepper or 1 whole bell pepper of any color

1 small onion diced

3 cloves of garlic minced

2 teaspoons chopped basil

1 tablespoon lemon juice

1 teaspoon turmeric

sea salt and pepper

1 slice of beet and parsley for garnish

extra virgin olive oil

Wash all the vegetables, dry and cut off the green tops. Clean the inside of the bell pepper, and dice into tiny pieces. Using a small amount of oil, sauté the onion and garlic till golden brown. Add turmeric. Add the bell pepper, sauté until tender. Add lemon juice, and stir. Turn into a bowl and set aside the mixture.

Chop the unpeeled eggplant in ½-inch pieces, and sprinkle with sea salt. Put the rest of the oil in a large skillet, and using high heat, sauté the eggplant until it has shrunk in size and is golden brown. Add the basil, mix in with the eggplant, and remove from heat. Let the eggplant sit in the skillet for about 5 minutes. It will excrete a tasty broth. Turn the eggplant and its broth to the bowl with the rest of the ingredients and mix.

Transfer to an artist plate and sprinkle with a little extra virgin olive oil. Garnish with a wedge of lime and a basil branch. Serve with a piece of artisan bread.

Be delicious!

Red Bean Starter Palette (Lubia Mazeh)

2 cups small red beans, or two cans of organic red beans drained

1 small onion cut in thin slices

¼ cup of rice vinegar (may be replaced with white or apple cider vinegar)

1 tablespoon lemon juice

1 tablespoon turmeric

1 teaspoon cinnamon

1 teaspoon Tabasco sauce

1 cup or one small can of organic tomato paste diluted in ½ cup of water

4 cups of water

sliced, pickled jalapeño for garnish

sea salt and pepper

olive oil

Wash the beans and soak over night. In an 8-inch saucepan using high heat, sauté onion in some olive oil until golden brown. Add turmeric and stir once or twice. Immediately add the diluted tomato paste and stir to mix. Add the vinegar and cinnamon to the sauce. Season to taste. Add the beans with 4 cups of water and cook over medium-low heat for 45 minutes. Note: If using canned beans, add only one cup of water with the beans and simmer for only 20 minutes. Stir occasionally. Cook until there is a thick consistency. Transfer to a bowl, and place the bowl on an artist plate. Sprinkle lemon juice and a little olive oil and garnish with jalapeño. Serve with a piece of rye artisan bread.

This dish may be served hot as lunch or dinner, or served cold as an appetizer.

Be delicious!

Chicken Sandwich with Pineapple Palette

1 pound boneless, skinless chicken thigh and breast

fresh squeezed juice from 1 large lemon

1 medium onion diced

¼ medium pineapple cut in ¼-inch thin slices

½ red onion cut in round thin slices

2 tablespoons finely chopped fresh tarragon

½ loaf of raisin bread cut in slices for sandwiches

2 tablespoons of cream cheese

¼ teaspoon cinnamon

grape seed oil

sea salt and pepper

Follow the Basic Chicken and Broth recipe. Remove chicken from broth and let it cool. Cut chicken into thin sandwich slices. Spread the cream cheese on raisin bread. Place the chicken on the bread and sprinkle a dash of cinnamon on the chicken, then add a slice of onion. Sprinkle on some tarragon, and add a layer of pineapple. Place another piece of bread with cream cheese on the sandwich. Cut in desired slices. Place on an artist plate and serve with sweet potato chips.

Be delicious!

Parishki Palette

- 1 pound ground beef or tofu substitute
- 1 small onion diced
- 3 cloves garlic minced
- 1 jalapeño finely chopped
- 1 medium tomato
- 1 cup of mixed red and yellow bell pepper
- 1 medium yam
- ½ cup parsley
- 1 tablespoon lemon juice
- 1 teaspoon turmeric
- 1 teaspoon cinnamon
- 1 package of either whole wheat thin flat bread or soft flour tortillas
- sea salt and pepper
- frying oil of choice
- toothpicks
- radishes for garnish

In a small saucepan, cook the yam in boiling water for 10 minutes or until soft. Once it is cool to the touch, dice the yam and set aside. In a large skillet, sauté the onion and garlic till golden. Add ground beef or tofu, stir and mix. Once the mixture is browned, add salt, pepper, cinnamon and turmeric and stir the mix until the spices are evenly distributed. Add bell pepper, tomato, yam and lemon juice and mix in the skillet. Season to taste. Remove from heat and mix in the parsley. Using a scooper, place 2 or 3 scoops in the center of a soft tortilla or flat bread. (It is important for the bread to be soft, or it will tear.) Fold in all the corners of the bread and secure with a toothpick. Deep fry or grill the parishkies in oil. You may also brush on some olive oil and broil them in the oven at 500° until the bread is slightly browned. Place the parishkies on an artist plate. Garnish with radishes. Serve with your favorite sauce or a side of Shirazi salad.

Be delicious!

Salads

One-a-Day Salad Palette

1 cup cottage cheese
3 cups baby spinach leaves
1 large tomato
1 large cucumber
½ cup shredded carrots
½ avocado
2 tablespoons of chopped green onion (may substitute with any type of onion)
½ cup fresh mint leaves
1 tablespoon fresh squeezed lemon juice
2 tablespoons walnuts (optional)
2 tablespoon extra virgin olive oil
sea salt and pepper
2 tablespoons toasted sesame seed

Wash and dry all the vegetables. Slice the avocado, cucumber and tomato into bite sizes. Sprinkle a little salt on the above vegetables, and toss the spinach and carrots. Transfer some of the vegetables to an artist plate. Sprinkle a little olive oil over it. In a small bowl, mix the cottage cheese, lemon juice, onion, walnuts and mint. Season to taste. Place the cottage cheese mix over the bed of salad on the artist plate. Serve with a piece of whole grain artisan bread.

I make this salad with whatever veggies I have in my refrigerator. Be creative ... just have one every day!

Be delicious!

Chicken and Potato Salad Palette (Salad Olvieh)

1 pound boneless, skinless chicken thigh and breast
4 eggs
1 cup green peas
2 large carrots
2 large russet potatoes
¼ cup mayonnaise

¼ cup fresh squeezed lemon juice
¼ cup extra virgin olive oil
1 medium onion diced
4 large, crunchy, dill-pickled cucumbers
sea salt and pepper
garnish: parsley, wedge of lemon and cherry tomatoes

In a medium saucepan, using medium-high heat, sauté the onion slightly till it wilts and glistens. Add chicken and brown with the onion. Season with sea salt and pepper and add 1 tablespoon of lemon juice. Reduce the heat to low. Cover the pan and let the chicken steam for 30 minutes. You may need to add 1 or 2 tablespoons of water depending on how hot your stove is and the type of pan you use. Remove from heat. Refrigerate to cool.

In separate pans, cook carrots, potatoes, peas and eggs with boiling water using medium heat till they are soft but before they lose their color. Remove from heat. Refrigerate to cool.

While the ingredients cool, create a simple sauce. In a bowl, mix the mayonnaise, lemon juice, olive oil, sea salt and pepper. Dice all the cooked vegetables (except the peas) and the pickled cucumbers separately. Be sure the potatoes are not so small that they get sticky. Put them in a large bowl. Remove the excess broth from the chicken, dice and shred. Add to the bowl. Pour the sauce over the chicken and thoroughly mix in with the vegetables.

Transfer to an artist plate. Garnish with the olives, cherry tomatoes, parsley and lemon wedge. Serve with sourdough bread.

Be delicious!

Shrimp Salad with Mango Palette

2 pounds peeled shrimp

1 firm mango

½ cup dry roasted peanuts

½ cup finely chopped cilantro

½ cup finely chopped mint leaves

½ cup shredded carrots

1 avocado

3 cloves garlic minced

2 tablespoons chopped red onion

fresh squeezed juice from 1 lime

½ teaspoon ginger

¼ cup soy sauce

¼ cup Seville orange juice or Mandarin orange juice

2 tablespoons sesame seed oil or extra virgin olive oil

sea salt and pepper

1 package brown rice noodles

In a small skillet, brown garlic and shrimp. Season to taste. Remove from heat and let cool. Slice the avocado and mango into ¼-inch pieces and put in a bowl. Add peanuts, shredded carrots, mint and cilantro. Cook the brown rice noodles according to the package instructions. When the noodles are drained, add a little extra virgin olive oil to it and allow to cool. Once the shrimp and noodles are cooled, put them in the bowl with the avocado and mango mixture. In a small bowl, mix lemon juice, soy sauce, oil, ginger and orange juice. Pour over the whole mixture and toss. Transfer to an artist plate, and sprinkle a little sesame oil over it.

Be delicious!

Romaine Lettuce Boat Palette

- 1 bunch romaine lettuce
- 1 pound ground chicken or diced tofu
- 1 medium, Red Delicious apple diced
- 1 medium onion diced
- ¼ cup white raisins
- ½ teaspoon ginger
- ½ teaspoon turmeric
- ½ teaspoon cinnamon
- 1 tablespoon finely chopped chives
- 1 tablespoon chopped, fresh lemongrass
- 1 tablespoon fresh squeezed lime juice
- 1 teaspoon honey
- 2 tablespoons orange juice
- 1 tablespoon soy sauce
- 2 tablespoons olive oil
- grape seed oil
- sea salt and pepper
- 1 wedge of lime for garnish

Separate the romaine lettuce leaves, and wash and dry them. In a small skillet, brown the onion and ground or diced chicken, and season to taste. Add the apples, white raisins, cinnamon and lime juice. Stir and sauté with the mix until the apples are slightly soft. Remove from heat. Add in the chives.

Sweet & Sour Sauce: In a small bowl, mix the orange juice, soy sauce, olive oil, honey and ginger.

Place the romaine lettuce leaves on an artist plate and spoon the mixture in the center of each leaf. Serve with a bit of sweet and sour sauce on the side. Garnish with a lime wedge.

Be delicious!

Butternut Squash with Pomegranate Palette

1 cup butternut squash, peeled and cut in ½ inch pieces
¼ cup crushed walnuts
½ cup pomegranate seeds
¼ cup chopped fresh basil
1 pound boneless, skinless chicken breast cut in 1-inch pieces
1 medium onion diced
2 tablespoons chopped red onion
½ ounce crumbled feta cheese

1 teaspoon cinnamon
fresh squeezed juice from 1 lemon
2 tablespoons pomegranate juice
1 teaspoon honey
grape seed oil
sea salt and pepper
a twig of tarragon for garnish

In a medium saucepan using medium-high heat, sauté the onion slightly till it wilts and glistens. Add chicken and brown with the onion. Season with sea salt and pepper and add 1 tablespoon of lemon juice. Reduce the heat to low. Cover the pan, and let the chicken steam for 30 minutes. You may need to add 1 or 2 tablespoons of water depending on how hot your stove is and the type of pan you use. Once the chicken is cooked, remove from heat and place in the refrigerator to cool. Brush the butternut squash with oil and sprinkle with a dash of salt and a dash of cinnamon. Place in a preheated oven at 400° for 20 minutes, or until lightly golden brown. After cooking, place the butternut squash on a cooling rack. Let cool to room temperature. In a cup, mix the rest of the lemon juice and pomegranate juice with the rest of the cinnamon, honey, sea salt and pepper. In a bowl, toss the chicken, butternut squash and the red onion and walnuts together. Place a layer of the mix leaves on an artist plate. Sprinkle with feta cheese and pomegranate seeds. Garnish with tarragon.

Be delicious!

Romaine and Bean Potato Salad Palette

1 bunch romaine lettuce

½ dry pinto beans, or 1 can organic pinto beans

4 eggs

2 medium potatoes

¼ cup thinly sliced red onion

fresh squeezed juice from 1 lemon

1 medium beet

extra virgin olive oil

1 tablespoon mayonnaise (preferably canola oil mayonnaise)

sea salt and pepper

Wash and dry the vegetables. Mix the lemon juice with 1 tablespoon of extra virgin olive oil. Add sea salt and pepper and mix in the red onions. Place in the refrigerator and let it soak for as long as your time allows, but no more than a day. Mix the mayonnaise with the rest of the lemon juice, olive oil, sea salt and pepper. Cook the pinto beans with a dash of salt with 1½ cups of water, over medium-low heat for an hour or until the beans are soft. Drain and let it cool. Hard boil the eggs. Once the eggs have cooled, use an egg cutter or cut them in rounds. Using part or all of the yolks is optional. In a small saucepan using medium-high heat, boil the potatoes. After the potatoes are cooked, set aside to cool. Once cooled, peel and cut them into 1-inch squares. Cook the beet by boiling it over medium heat for about 25 minutes, or until it is soft to the fork. After the beet is cooked, let it cool, peel and cut into 2-inch wedges (you may also use canned beet). Chop the romaine lettuce leaves into 2-inch pieces. Put all the dry ingredients, except for the beet in a salad bowl. Add in the soaked onions. Pour the mayonnaise sauce to the mix, and toss to evenly spread throughout the salad. Place the salad on an artist plate. Arrange the beet on the side as a nutritional garnish. Serve with a piece of rye artisan bread.

Be delicious!

Light Entrées

Savory Meat Pie Palette

1 pound lean ground beef
2 cups sliced mushrooms
½ cup finely chopped parsley
1 medium onion diced
1 teaspoon curry powder
fresh squeezed juice from 1 lemon
2 tablespoon oat flour (or unsweetened oat meal)
ready made whole grain pie shell
extra virgin olive oil
sea salt and pepper
one sliced round tomato
Parmesan cheese for garnish

Sauté the mushrooms. When finished sautéing, mix in half the lemon juice and set aside. In a skillet, brown sauté onion over high heat till golden brown. Add meat and season to taste till the meat browns. Reduce the heat to medium. Add the mushrooms, parsley, rest of the juice and the curry powder to the mix and stir. Add the oat flour to the mix. This will thicken the mixture to a pasty consistency so that it can be the in the pie crust. Sprinkle a generous amount of Parmesan cheese and arrange the tomato slices on top. Season the tomatoes. Put the mixture in the whole grain pie shell. Bake in the center of a preheated oven for 25 minutes with a temperature of 375° or until the crust is browned. Let the pie cool slightly. Serve a big piece on an artist plate with a side of Shirazi salad, olives and your favorite pickled veggies.

Be delicious!

Cutlet Palette (Kotlet)

1 pound ground beef, ground turkey or ground chicken
2 large russet potatoes
1 small onion grated
2 eggs
1 cup bread crumbs
¼ cup grape seed oil

½ teaspoon cinnamon
½ teaspoon turmeric
1 teaspoon saffron solution (see Cooking Tips & Notes)
garnish: cherry tomatoes, dill pickled cucumber and parsley

Tomato Sauce (optional)

3 cups of tomato juice or canned tomato sauce
¼ cup minced onion
½ teaspoon turmeric
fresh juice of one large lime or lemon
½ teaspoon minced garlic
olive oil

Cutlet: Boil the potatoes in a medium saucepan. Let them cool to the touch, then peel, mash and transfer to a mixing bowl. Season with salt. Add the meat, onion, spices, eggs and saffron solution. Knead the mixture until all the ingredients are perfectly incorporated. You need to pull up your sleeves and use your hands for this one! Especially if you are preparing the recipe with ground chicken. It becomes a little sticky. In a tray, cover the surface with bread crumbs. Using a scooper, pick up pieces of the mix (as much as the palm of your hand). Make a little ball first, and then flatten the cutlet into oval-shaped patties. Lay them on the tray with bread crumbs. Once all the mix has been shaped and placed on the tray, sprinkle them with more bread crumbs to get them breaded on both sides. In a nonstick skillet, place the oil and heat it for 30 seconds. Arrange the cutlets on the skillet. Turn the heat to medium and brown each side of the cutlets.

Tomato Sauce: In a separate skillet, brown onion in some olive oil, add turmeric and stir. Add lime juice and tomato sauce and garlic. Season to taste. Simmer for five minutes. Transfer cutlets to an artist plate and garnish with cherry tomatoes, pickled cucumber, parsley and cherry tomatoes.

Serve the tomato sauce over the cutlet or on the side of cutlets. Serve flat bread, or saffron rice and a side of salad Shirazi.

Be delicious!

Herbal Meatballs Palette (Kufteh)

1 pound ground beef
1 cup finely chopped fresh parsley
1 cup finely chopped fresh cilantro
1 cup finely chopped fresh chives or the greens of green onions
¼ cup chopped fresh mint leaves
¼ cup chopped fresh basil leaves
¼ cup chopped fresh dill

¼ cup finely chopped fresh tarragon
2 medium onions diced
2 eggs
½ cup rice
½ cup yellow split peas
2 tablespoons dried summer savory
1 cup prunes or dried seedless plums
fresh squeezed juice of 1 lime or lemon

1 cup tomato juice
1 teaspoon cinnamon
1 teaspoon turmeric
two teaspoons saffron solution (see Cooking Tips & Notes)
1 cup cherry tomatoes

In a medium saucepan, cook rice and split peas over medium heat for 25 minutes. Let it cool to the touch. Remove the liquid from the mix and combine with tomato juice, lemon juice, ½ teaspoon cinnamon, ½ teaspoon turmeric, sea salt and pepper. In a small skillet, brown half of the diced onion over medium-high heat. Add the prunes and stir in with the onion. Add half of the saffron solution and mix well so the saffron reaches evenly. Remove from heat, and let it cool. In a big mixing bowl, combine all the herbs, meat, drained and cooled rice, yellow split peas, salt, pepper and the rest of the saffron solution, cinnamon and turmeric. Knead the mixture until all ingredients are perfectly incorporated. You need to pull up your sleeve and use your hands for this one! Scoop up a ball as big as the palm of your hand. Flatten it a little and place a spoonful of prune and onion mixture in the center. Then wrap the prune and form a ball around it.

In a large saucepan, brown the rest of the onion. Add the tomato juice mixture, bring to a boil, and then reduce the heat to medium. Start gently placing the meatballs into the simmering saucepan. Cover the saucepan and reduce the heat so the saucepan does not boil over. After 30 minutes of simmering, add the cherry tomatoes (optional). Simmer for another 20 minutes. Transfer to an artist plate, serve with flat bread and a bit of plain yogurt.

Be delicious!

Chicken and Pine Nut Meatballs Palette

1 pound of ground chicken
1 cup finely chopped roasted pine nuts
½ tablespoon finely minced fresh oregano
¼ cup chopped fresh basil
1 cup grated onions
3 cloves garlic minced
½ teaspoon cinnamon
½ teaspoon turmeric
1 teaspoon oregano powder
fresh squeezed juice of 1 lime or lemon
1 cup tomato juice
sea salt and pepper
extra virgin olive oil
2 tablespoons grated Parmesan cheese
1 package of your favorite pasta

In a medium saucepan, put 2 tablespoons olive oil and heat for 30 seconds. Add half of the grated onion. Once the onion starts to brown, add the tomato and lemon juice, minced garlic, oregano, sea salt and pepper. Bring to a boil, and then reduce to low heat. In a mixing bowl, put chicken, oregano powder, pine nuts, half of the grated onions, cinnamon, turmeric, sea salt and pepper. Knead chicken till all the ingredients are incorporated. Make 1-inch balls from the mix and gently put inside the simmering sauce. Cover and cook over medium-low heat for 30 minutes. Remove from heat and add basil and oregano. And gently stir in the sauce. Prepare some pasta according to the instructions on the package. Place the pasta on an artist plate. Put some of the meatballs and sauce over the pasta. Sprinkle Parmesan cheese over it. Serve with a slice of ciabatta bread

Be delicious!

Stuffed Bell Peppers Palette (Dolmeh phelphel)

1 pound ground beef, turkey or chicken
6 medium bell pepper of various colors
1 jalapeño pepper
1 cup finely chopped fresh parsley
1 cup finely chopped fresh cilantro
1 cup finely chopped fresh chives or the greens of green onions

¼ cup chopped fresh mint leaves
¼ cup chopped fresh basil leaves
¼ cup chopped fresh dill
¼ cup finely chopped fresh tarragon
2 medium onions diced
½ cup rice
½ cup yellow split peas

½ cup tomato paste
2 tablespoons vinegar
fresh squeezed juice of 1 lime or lemon
1 cup tomato juice
1 teaspoon cinnamon
1 teaspoon turmeric
saffron solution (see Cooking Tips & Notes)

In a medium saucepan, cook rice and split peas over medium heat for 25 minutes. Let cool to the touch. Remove the liquid from the mix and combine with tomato juice, vinegar, ½ teaspoon cinnamon, ½ teaspoon turmeric, sea salt and pepper. Then reduce the heat to keep warm. Dilute the tomato paste in ½ cup water. In a small skillet, brown half of the diced onion and meat over medium-high heat. Add in the rest of the cinnamon and turmeric. Stir in all the herbs, rice and yellow split peas. Add the diluted tomato paste. Cover, reduce heat to low, and let it steam for 10 minutes. Remove from heat, stir the mixture once, and let it cool to the touch. Wash and dry bell peppers. Cut the top part of the bell pepper ½-inch below the green stem. Empty the inside of the seeds. Stuff bell peppers with the mixture. Use a toothpick to secure them. Arrange in saucepan. Poke a hole on the jalapeño pepper and put in the saucepan. Pour the tomato juice sauce in the saucepan around the peppers. Bring to a boil. Quickly reduce heat to medium-low. Simmer for 45 minutes. Arrange stuffed peppers on an artist plate. Serve with flat bread and a bit of plain yogurt.

Be delicious!

Eve's Stuffed Apples Palette (Dolmeh Sib)

1 pound filet of beef diced into ¼-inch pieces

1 medium onion diced

5 large Red Delicious apples

½ cup white raisins (optional)

1 cup yellow split peas

fresh squeezed juice of 1 lime or lemon

2 teaspoons cinnamon

1 teaspoon turmeric

2 teaspoons saffron solution (see Cooking Tips & Notes)

1 ounce melted butter

grape seed oil

sea salt and pepper

Wash and dry all the apples. Cut the tops of 4 apples just ½-inch below the top. Using a scooper, empty the inside of the apples. Brush the insides with butter and sprinkle with half of the cinnamon and a dash of salt. Dice the other apple into very small pieces (less than ¼-inch and bigger than minced size). In a small saucepan, cook the yellow split peas by boiling in two cups of water and a dash of salt for 30 minutes over medium-low heat. Drain and let it cool. In a small skillet, brown half of the diced onion and meat over medium-high heat. Add in the rest of the cinnamon and turmeric. Remove from heat, set aside. In a separate skillet, sauté the apples with ½ tablespoon of oil and butter. Add the raisins. Sprinkle with lemon juice. Gently toss the apples' meat, drained peas and saffron solution together. Stuff the apples with the mixture and secure the apples with a toothpick. Bake in the center of a preheated oven at 400° for about 20 minutes or until the flesh of the apple is soft to fork. Transfer to an artist plate. Serve with a side of saffron rice and plain yogurt.

Be delicious!

Stuffed Acorn Squash Palette

1 cup adzuki beans (or two cans of organic adzuki beans drained)

2 medium acorn squash

1 medium onion diced

½ cup finely chopped green onions

1 cup finely chopped celery

1 cup shredded carrots

½ cup finely chopped fresh cilantro

1 teaspoon ginger

grape seed oil

sea salt and pepper

1 ounce crumbled feta cheese (optional)

Wash and dry the acorn squash. Cut off a thin layer of skin from each end. Cut them in half and clean the inside by scooping out the seed. Wash them again. Brush the squash with oil and sprinkle with half of the cinnamon, and a dash of salt. Bake in the center of a preheated oven 400° for 25 minutes, or until the squash begins to slightly brown. In a small saucepan, cook the (uncooked and washed) adzuki beans with 2 cups of water, over medium-low heat for one hour. Drain.

In a small skillet, brown the onions, celery and carrots. Add cinnamon, ginger, sea salt and pepper. Add the beans and the cilantro to the skillet and remove from heat. Stir the mix making sure all the ingredients are evenly spread. Stuff the baked squash. Transfer to an artist plate and sprinkle with feta cheese crumbles.

Be delicious!

Skillet Kabob Palette

1½ pounds ground beef, chicken or turkey

1 medium onion grated

½ teaspoon cinnamon

1 teaspoon sumac

2 teaspoons saffron solution (see Cooking Tips & Notes)

grape seed oil

sea salt and pepper

½ bell pepper cut in 2-inch pieces

½ cup cherry tomatoes

basil leaf

In a mixing bowl, knead meat, salt, pepper, cinnamon and onion until all the ingredients are mixed. Spread over a medium, nonstick skillet covering the whole skillet like a giant hamburger. Place over the stove using high heat. Once the skillet heats up and the patty starts to lift, cut the patty with a nonstick spatula in half. This will release the pressure, and the patty will start to cook from the center. Cut the two halves of the patty into 1-inch stripes. Using a tong, turn over the strips so that the other side gets browned. Reduce the heat to medium-low. Spread the tomatoes and the bell pepper over the tomatoes. Once browned, remove and place on an artist plate. Garnish with the bell pepper and cherry tomatoes from the skillet and the basil twig. Sprinkle with a dash of sumac. Serve with flat bread.

Be delicious!

Mahi (Fish) Kabob Palette

2 pounds salmon or any other fish for grilling (cut in 2-inch pieces if desired)

1 medium onion grated

3 cloves of garlic minced

½ cup Seville orange juice or ¼ cup lemon juice plus ¼ cup orange juice

2 teaspoons saffron solution (see Cooking Tips & Notes)

extra virgin olive oil

salt and pepper

juice of one fresh lemon

basil twig

Marinate the fish with onion, salt, pepper, Seville orange or orange/lemon juice, olive oil, garlic and saffron solution in the refrigerator for one hour. If using metal skewers, brush or spray them with oil. Skew the fish on the skewers. Grill on high heat to the desired tenderness. Use a slice of pita bread to separate the fish from the hot skewer. Place over flat bread on an artist plate. Serve with a side of salad Shirazi and spring herbal rice. Garnish with basil.

Be delicious!

Omelets and Egg Dishes

Eggplant Omelet Palette

1 medium eggplant
2 cloves garlic minced
¼ cup Parmesan cheese
5 eggs
½ tablespoon dried mint
1 tablespoon saffron solution (see Cooking Tips & Notes)
sea salt and pepper
extra virgin oil

Wash and remove the green top from the eggplant. Peel and cut into thin, 1-inch slices. Spray with oil and sprinkle a dash of salt. Spread garlic all over the oiled eggplant. In a large skillet, heat 3 tablespoons of oil and lay the eggplant on the skillet. Spread the garlic all over the eggplant. Brown both sides on medium-high heat. In a mixing bowl, whisk eggs, Parmesan cheese, salt, pepper and saffron solution together. Pour egg mix over the browned eggplant. Cover and steam till the eggs harden. Remove from heat. Serve on an artist plate with a slice of buttered toast. Garnish with a dash of dried mint.

Be delicious!

Date Omelet Palette

1 cup de-seeded dates diced in small bite-sizes
5 eggs
½ teaspoon cinnamon
½ teaspoon saffron solution (see Cooking Tips & Notes)
sea salt
½ tablespoons butter
grape seed oil

In a mixing bowl, whisk eggs, a dash of salt and saffron solution together. Add dates and mix. In a medium skillet, heat butter and 1 tablespoon grape seed oil over medium-high heat. Pour the mix on the skillet. Cover and steam till the eggs harden. Remove from heat. Serve on an artist plate with a slice of buttered toast. Garnish with a dash of cinnamon.

This omelet is known to be an aphrodisiac for men!

Be delicious!

Tomato Basil Omelet Palette

2 medium Roma tomatoes cut into circles
¼ finely chopped green onions
1 clove garlic minced
¼ cup finely chopped fresh basil
5 eggs
sea salt and pepper
2 tablespoons extra virgin olive oil
black olives

In a mixing bowl, whisk eggs, a dash of sea salt and pepper together. Add basil. In a medium skillet, heat oil over medium-high heat. Mix the green onion, garlic and tomatoes. Neatly put in the skillet making sure all the juice, garlic and onion enters the skillet. Brown tomatoes on each side. Pour the whisked egg and basil mix over the browned tomatoes. Cover and steam till eggs harden. Remove from heat. Serve on an artist plate with a slice of sesame flat bread and black olives.

Be delicious!

Dill and Potato Omelet Palette

2 small red potatoes washed and diced
½ tablespoon dill
1 clove garlic, minced
½ teaspoon cinnamon
5 eggs
sea salt and pepper
2 tablespoons extra virgin olive oil

In a mixing bowl, whisk eggs, a dash of sea salt and pepper together. Add garlic and dill and mix well. In a medium skillet, sauté potatoes with half of the oil and a dash of salt over medium-high heat. Reduce the heat, cover and let potatoes steam cook. Pour egg/dill mix over potatoes. Cover again and allow eggs to harden. Remove from heat. Serve on an artist plate with a side of saffron rice and a little yogurt.

Be delicious!

Asparagus Kukoo Palette

3 cups chopped, washed and dried asparagus

¼ cup grated onion

5 eggs

¼ cup oat flour or unsweetened oat meal

1 clove garlic, mince

½ teaspoon turmeric

5 eggs

sea salt and pepper

½ teaspoon saffron solution (see Cooking Tips & Notes)

4 tablespoons extra virgin olive oil

½ tomato cut into wedges

In a mixing bowl, whisk eggs, a dash of salt, pepper, oat and turmeric together. Add asparagus, onion and garlic to the mix and beat well. In a large nonstick oven skillet, heat oil over medium-high heat. Pour the mixture slowly but steadily onto the skillet so that it covers the skillet evenly. Reduce the heat. Once the mix starts to brown on the edges and the surface appears to be hardening, transfer to the center of a preheated (400°) oven and bake until the top is golden brown. Remove from oven. Cut in triangular shaped pieces and serve on an artist plate. Garnish with tomato wedges. This makes a great side dish for steaks.

This is a great breakfast for the morning after drinking and partying. It helps with hangovers!

Be delicious!

Potato Kukoo Palette

3 large potatoes, washed and peeled
¼ cup grated onion
5 eggs
½ teaspoon turmeric
5 eggs
sea salt and pepper
½ teaspoon saffron solution (see Cooking Tips & Notes)
4 tablespoons extra virgin olive oil
few branches of seasonal herbs

Cook the potato in a saucepan until soft to fork. Remove water and put in a mixing bowl and smash till smooth. Add in grated onion, salt, pepper, cinnamon, saffron solution and crack the eggs on the mix. Beat the mixture till all the ingredients are mixed. In a large, nonstick, oven skillet, heat oil over medium-high heat. Pour the mixture slowly, but steadily, onto the skillet so that it covers the skillet evenly. Reduce the heat. Once the mix starts to brown on the edges and the surface appears to be hardening, transfer to the center of a preheated (400°) oven and bake until the top is golden brown. Cut in square pieces. Serve on an artist plate with yogurt or pickles. Garnish with herbs and pickles.

Be delicious!

Grilled Eggplant and Tomato Omelet Palette
(Mira Ghassemi)

2 medium eggplants
2 large tomatoes
5 whole cloves of garlic
5 eggs
1 teaspoon turmeric
sea salt and pepper
½ teaspoon saffron solution (see Cooking Tips & Notes)
fresh juice of half a lime
extra virgin olive oil
2 ½ cups water
2 ounces smoked white fish (optional)
wedge of lemon

Wash and dry eggplants and tomatoes. Slit the eggplants in two places. This is to avoid the steam getting trapped in them. Grill the eggplants and tomatoes over an open grill on medium-high heat. When the eggplants and tomatoes are cooked and their skin is partially caramelized, remove from heat and place on a cutting board. When they are cool enough to touch, remove the skin, place with garlic and chop together with the grilled and peeled eggplant. Chop the grilled tomatoes. Heat oil in a skillet over high heat. Add turmeric to the oil. Add chopped eggplant and garlic. Add chopped tomato with all its juice. Add lime juice, salt and pepper. Stir to mix all the ingredients evenly. Crack the eggs gently on various corners of the skillet. Using a wooden spatula, just break the yolks and slightly mix with its surrounding ingredients. The mixing of the eggs must remain uneven. Once the eggs are poached, season to taste. Serve on a bed of saffron rice with a slice of smoked fish on the side of an artist plate. Garnish with a wedge of lemon.

Be delicious!

Khoresh

Gourmet of Filet, Parsley, Chives and Fenugreek Palette (Qorrmet Sabzi)

- 1 ½ pound fillet of beef cut in 1-inch pieces
- 1 cup kidney beans washed
- 3 cups fresh parsley finely chopped
- 1 cup fresh chives finely chopped
- 1 large onion diced
- 2 tablespoon dried fenugreek
- 4 whole dried Persian limes or fresh squeezed juice of 2 limes
- 1 teaspoon turmeric
- 1 teaspoon saffron solution (see Cooking Tips & Notes)
- ingredients for a side of saffron rice (see Basic Saffron Rice)
- 3 cups of water
- sea salt and pepper
- grape seed oil

Wash and soak the beans. In a large saucepan, heat 1 tablespoon of oil and brown sauté the onion till golden. Add turmeric and stir. Add meat and brown with the onion. Season to taste. Drain washed beans and add to the saucepan. Add 3 cups of water and bring to boil. Then reduce the heat to medium-low, cover and let it simmer for 40 minutes or until the beans are almost cooked. In a large skillet, sauté parsley, chives and fenugreek with 2 tablespoons of oil over high heat until the herbs reduce and wilt.

Add the herbs and the Persian limes or lime juice. Adjust the taste by adding more salt if needed. Stir and cover again, let it simmer over medium-low heat, stirring occasionally.

After 40 more minutes, check to see if the beans and meat are cooked through, then stir in saffron solution. On an artist plate, place some saffron rice and serve the Qorrmet over it.

Be delicious!

Gourmet of Fillet, Parsley, Mint and Celery Palette (Khoresh-e-Karafs)

1 ½ pound fillet of beef cut in 1-inch pieces

3 cups fresh parsley finely chopped

1 cup fresh mint finely chopped

2 cups celery washed and cut in 1-inch pieces

1 large onion diced

fresh squeezed juice of 2 limes

1 teaspoon turmeric

1 teaspoon saffron solution (see Cooking Tips & Notes)

ingredients for a side of saffron rice (see Basic Saffron Rice)

3 cups of water

sea salt and pepper

grape seed oil

1 ½ cup water

In a large saucepan, heat 1 tablespoon oil and brown sauté the onion till golden, add turmeric and stir. Add meat and brown with the onion. Season to taste. Add water and bring to a boil. Reduce heat to medium-low and simmer for 20 minutes. In a large skillet, sauté parsley, mint with 2 tablespoons of oil over high heat until the herbs reduce and wilt. Set aside on a plate. In the same skillet, sauté the celery until it is golden and glistens. Put the herbs and celery and lemon juice in the saucepan over the meat and stir. Cover and let it simmer over medium-low heat, stirring occasionally. After 40 more minutes, check to see if the meat and celery are cooked through then stir in saffron solution. On an artist plate, place some saffron rice and serve the Khoresh over it.

Be delicious!

Gourmet of Chicken and Eggplant Palette (Khoresh-e-Bademjan)

1 ½ pound boneless, skinless chicken breast and thigh cut into 2-inch pieces

2 medium eggplants or 4 small Japanese eggplants

4 medium Roma tomatoes, washed and peeled

1 large onion diced

fresh squeezed juice of 2 limes

1 teaspoon turmeric

1 teaspoon cinnamon

1 teaspoon saffron solution (see Cooking Tips & Notes)

ingredients for a side of saffron rice (see Basic Saffron Rice)

1 cup water

sea salt and pepper

grape seed oil

Wash and peel eggplants. Sprinkle with salt. Fill a large saucepan with water and bring to a boil. Remove from heat. Add the eggplants to the boiling water. Boil eggplants for 5 minutes, and then drain the water. In a large skillet, brown the eggplants in some extra virgin olive oil and set aside. In a large saucepan, heat 1 tablespoon oil and brown sauté the onion till golden, add turmeric and stir. Add chicken and brown with the onion. Season to taste. Add half of the lemon juice and water, stir to mix. Reduce heat to medium-low, cover and cook for 20 minutes. Mix the rest of the lemon juice with cinnamon and saffron solution. Lay the eggplant and tomatoes over the chicken. Pour the lemon juice mix over the saucepan. Stir gently to mix. Cover and cook for another 20 minutes over medium-low heat. On an artist plate, place some saffron rice and serve the Khoresh over it. When available, I like to replace lime juice with sour grapes. They are available in the summer months in local import food stores. Sauté and use in place of lime juice.

Be delicious!

Gourmet Beef, Bell Pepper And Coconut Ginger Sauce Palette (Khoresh-e-Felfel)

- 1 ½ pounds fillet of beef, cut in 1-inch pieces
- 2 bell peppers cut in 1-inch squares
- 1 cup tomato sauce
- 2 cups coconut milk
- 1 chili pepper
- 1 teaspoon chili powder
- 1 large onion diced
- fresh squeezed juice of 1 lime
- 1 teaspoon turmeric
- 1 teaspoon cinnamon
- 1 teaspoon ginger
- 1 teaspoon saffron solution (see Cooking Tips & Notes)
- ingredients for a side of saffron rice (see Basic Saffron Rice)
- 1 cup water
- sea salt and pepper
- grape seed oil

In a medium skillet, sauté bell pepper with a dash of salt and a tablespoon of oil and set aside. In a large saucepan, heat 1 tablespoon of oil and brown sauté the onion till golden, add turmeric and stir. Add meat and brown with the onion. Season to taste. Add lemon juice, tomato sauce, salt and pepper. Stir to mix. Reduce heat to medium-low, cover and cook for 20 minutes. Add bell pepper. Mix in coconut juice, cinnamon, ginger and saffron solution. Season to taste. Cover and cook for another 20 minutes over medium-low heat. On an artist plate, spoon saffron rice and serve the Khoresh over it.

Note: This dish looks particularly beautiful when using multiple colors of bell pepper. For example, ½ red, ½ green, ½ yellow and ½ orange.

Be delicious!

Gourmet of Chicken with Walnuts and Pomegranate Sauce Palette (Khoresh-e-Fesenjoon)

1 ½ pounds boneless, skinless chicken breast and thigh cut in 2-inch pieces

3 cups finely crushed walnuts

1 cup butternut squash cut in 1-inch pieces

2 cups pomegranate paste or 4 cups of pomegranate juice (See Pomegranate Paste)

¼ cup sugar in the raw

1 large onion diced

fresh squeezed juice of 1 lemon

1 teaspoon cinnamon

1 teaspoon saffron solution (see Cooking Tips & Notes)

ingredients for a side of saffron rice (see Basic Saffron Rice)

1 cup water

sea salt and pepper

grape seed oil

garnish: pomegranate seeds

If you are not using pomegranate juice, follow the Pomegranate Paste recipe. Brown butternut squash in oil, season with salt and set aside. In a saucepan, combine crushed walnuts, cinnamon, pomegranate paste, a dash of salt and 3 cups of water. Gently bring to a boil, stirring occasionally. Reduce heat to low, cover and simmer for 35 minutes, stirring occasionally. In a large saucepan, heat 1 tablespoon oil and brown sauté the onion till golden. Add chicken and brown with the onion. Season to taste. Add half of the lemon juice and ¼ cup water, stir to mix. Reduce heat to medium-low, cover and cook for 25 minutes. Put the walnut and pomegranate mix over chicken. Add sugar and saffron solution. Mix it in. Add butternut squash (save some for garnish). Simmer for 15 minutes over medium-low heat stirring occasionally. On an artist plate, place saffron rice and serve the Khoresh over it. Garnish with pomegranate seeds and butternut squash.

Pomegranate paste is a dark, maroon color. When mixed and cooked with walnuts, the sauce will have a dark, reddish, brown color.

Be delicious!

Gourmet of Beef and Quince Palette (Khoresh-e-beh)

1½ pounds beef fillet cut in ¼-inch pieces

2 fresh quince

½ cup yellow split peas

1 large onion diced

fresh squeezed juice of 1 lemon

¼ cup tomato paste

4 tablespoon melted butter

1 teaspoon turmeric

1 teaspoon cinnamon

1 teaspoon saffron solution (see Cooking Tips & Notes)

ingredients for a side of saffron rice (see Basic Saffron Rice)

1 cup water

sea salt and pepper

grape seed oil

Wash, polish and cut the quinces in 2-inch wedges. In a large skillet, brown both sides of the quince wedges in half oil/half butter. Set aside. In a large saucepan, heat 1 tablespoon of oil and brown sauté the onion till golden, add turmeric and stir. Add meat and brown with the onion. Season to taste. Add yellow split peas and water, stir to mix. Reduce heat to medium-low, cover and cook for 30 minutes. Mix lemon juice with cinnamon and saffron solution, tomato paste and ¼ cup water. Lay the browned quince over the meat and peas. Pour the lemon juice, tomato paste and spice mix over the saucepan. Pour in the rest of the butter. Stir gently to mix. Cover and cook for another 30 minutes over medium-low heat. On an artist plate, place saffron rice and serve the Khoresh over it.

Be delicious!

Gourmet of Fillet and Okra Palette (Khoresh-e-Bamieh)

1½ pounds beef fillet or stew meat cut in ½-inch pieces

½ pound fresh okra, washed and dried

2 medium Roma tomatoes diced

½ cup yellow split peas

1 large onion diced

fresh squeezed juice of 1 lemon

1 teaspoon turmeric

1 teaspoon cinnamon

1 teaspoon saffron solution (see Cooking Tips & Notes)

ingredients for a side of saffron rice (see Basic Saffron Rice)

1 cup water

sea salt and pepper

grape seed oil

In a large skillet, brown okra in extra virgin olive oil and set aside. In the same skillet, quickly sauté diced tomatoes over high heat. Set aside. In a large saucepan, heat 1 tablespoon oil and brown sauté the onion till golden. Add turmeric and stir. Add meat and brown with the onion. Season to taste. Add yellow split peas and water, stir to mix. Reduce heat to medium-low, cover and cook for 30 minutes. Mix lemon juice with cinnamon and saffron solution. Lay the sauté okra and tomatoes over the meat and peas. Pour the lemon juice mix over the saucepan. Stir gently to mix. Cover and cook for another 20 minutes over medium-low heat. On an artist plate, place some saffron rice and serve the Khoresh over it.

Be delicious!

Rice Dishes

Chicken Kabob and Saffron Rice Palette

2 Cornish hens cut in pieces
2 tablespoons rosemary (optional)
1 medium onion grated
3 cloves of garlic minced
6 Roma tomatoes cut in halves
2 tablespoons saffron solution (see Cooking Tips & Notes)
extra virgin olive oil
sea salt and pepper
juice of one fresh lemon
basil twig

Marinate the chicken with onion, salt, pepper, lemon juice, olive oil, garlic, saffron solution and rosemary. Place in the refrigerator for one hour. If using metal skewers, brush or spray them with some oil. Skew the chicken on the skewers. Skew the tomatoes on two skewers. Grill on high heat to the desired tenderness. Use a slice of pita bread to separate the chicken from the hot skewer. Place over flat bread on an artist plate. Serve with a side of salad Shirazi and saffron rice. Garnish with basil.

Be delicious!

Lentil Rice with Raisins and Date Palette (Adas Polo)

2 cups long grain white or brown Basmati rice

1 cup lentils, or 2 cans of organic lentils drained

1 cup raisins

½ cup dates, de-seeded cut into bite-size pieces

1 cup diced onion

2 teaspoons cinnamon

1 tablespoon sea salt

4 cups water

5 tablespoons grape seed oil or any other flavorless cooking oil

3 tablespoons butter (optional)

2 teaspoons saffron solution (see Cooking Tips & Notes)

ingredients for the Basic Chicken

Wash lentils and place them in a small pot with 1½ cups water and a dash of salt. Bring to a boil, and then reduce the heat to medium-low and simmer for 20 minutes. Drain and set aside. Wash and drain the rice. Put the water and salt in a medium-sized saucepan, and bring to a boil. Add rice. Stir once. Reduce the heat to medium-high so the saucepan does not boil over. After 5 minutes the rice becomes longer in length and starts swimming in the simmering water. Before the rice gets sticky, drain the water by emptying the saucepan over a colander. Wash and dry the saucepan. Grease the bottom of the saucepan with a little butter, and add a little oil to it. Put a layer of rice back to the saucepan and then a layer of lentil and a dash of cinnamon all over it. Continue the layering until no more rice or lentils are left. Melt a little butter and add half of the saffron solution to it. Pour in a circular form in the center of the rice and spread it by gently fluffing the rice around the solution. Pour the rest of the oil all over the rice. Place a clean towel over the saucepan and firmly press the lid onto the pan, securing the towel. Steam for 20 minutes for white rice and 30 minutes for brown rice.

In a skillet, brown onion with a 1 tablespoon of butter and 1 tablespoon oil. Add raisins and 1 teaspoon saffron solution. Turn rice on a serving platter and fluff out the rice. Push the dates inside and around the rice. Sprinkle the raisin on the rice. Serve on an artist platter with piece of basic chicken, a dash of cinnamon and some yogurt.

Be delicious!

Shish Kabob and Saffron Rice Palette

3 pounds filet of beef cut in 2-inch pieces

1 medium onion grated

1 onion cut in 2-inch pieces

1 medium green bell pepper washed and cut in 2 pieces

6 Roma tomatoes cut in halves

1 teaspoon cinnamon

2 tablespoons saffron solution (see Cooking Tips & Notes)

extra virgin olive oil

sea salt and pepper

juice of one fresh lemon

basil twig

tarragon

red radish

Marinate the meat with onion, salt, pepper, lemon juice, olive oil, saffron solution and cinnamon. Place in the refrigerator for one hour. If using metal skewers, brush or spray them with some oil. Skew the meat on the skewers. In between the pieces of meat put slices of onion and bell pepper. Skew the tomatoes on two skewers. Grill on high heat to the desired tenderness. Use a slice of pita bread to separate the meat from the hot skewer. Place over flat bread on an artist plate. Serve with a side of salad Shirazi. Garnish with basil and tarragon.

Be delicious!

Spring Herbal Rice (Sabzi Polo)

2 cups long grain white or brown Basmati rice
1 cup finely chopped parsley
1 cup finely chopped cilantro
½ cup finely chopped chives
garlic clove
¼ cup finely chopped dill
¼ cup finely chopped basil
1 tablespoon dry summer savory

3 tablespoon minced
1 teaspoon cinnamon
1 tablespoon sea salt
4 cups water
grape seed oil
2 tablespoon butter (optional)
1 tablespoon saffron solution (see Cooking Tips & Notes)

Toss all the herbs and garlic together and set aside. Wash and drain the rice.

Put the water and salt in a medium saucepan, and bring to a boil. Add rice. Stir once. Reduce the heat to medium-high so the saucepan does not boil over. After 5 minutes, the rice becomes longer in length and starts swimming in the simmering water. Before the rice gets sticky, drain the water by emptying the saucepan over a colander. Wash and dry the saucepan. Grease the bottom of the saucepan with a little butter, and add a little oil to it. Return the rice back to the saucepan one layer at the time. In between each layer, sprinkle 2 cups of the fresh herbs. Spread it over rice evenly. Melt a little butter and add the saffron solution to it. Pour in a circular form in the center of the rice and spread it by gently fluffing the rice around the solution. Pour the rest of the oil all over the rice. Place a clean towel over the saucepan and firmly press the lid onto the saucepan, securing the towel. Steam for 20 minutes for white rice and 30 minutes for brown rice. Turn over on a serving platter. Place rice on an artist plate with a piece of roasted beef from the Basic Beef recipe in the center. Sprinkle with a dash of cinnamon.

Serve with a side of Mahi Kabob. Use Mandarin or Seville oranges for garnish.

Be delicious!

Saffron Rice with Barberries Palette (Zereshk Polo)

- 2 cups long grain white or brown Basmati rice
- ½ cup barberries
- 1 tablespoon sugar in the raw or regular sugar
- ½ teaspoon cinnamon
- 1 tablespoon sea salt
- 4 cups water
- 4 tablespoons grape seed oil or any other flavorless cooking oil
- 2 tablespoons butter (optional)
- 1 teaspoon saffron solution (see Cooking Tips & Notes)
- 1 tablespoon raw pistachio rinds
- 1 tablespoon fresh orange rind
- If using chicken, include ingredients for Basic Cooked Chicken

Wash and drain the rice. Put the water and salt in a medium saucepan, and bring to a boil. Add rice. Stir once. Reduce the heat to medium-high so the saucepan does not boil over. After 5 minutes, the rice will become longer in length and will start swimming in the simmering water. Before the rice gets sticky, drain the water by emptying the saucepan over a colander. Wash the saucepan and dry. Grease the bottom of the saucepan with a little butter. And add a little oil to it. Return the rice back to the saucepan. Melt a little butter and add the saffron solution to it. Pour in a circular form in the center of the rice and spread it by gently fluffing the rice around the solution. Pour the rest of the oil all over the rice. Place a clean towel over the saucepan and firmly press the lid onto the saucepan, securing the towel. Steam for 20 minutes for white rice and 30 minutes for brown rice. Turn over on a serving platter. If you use a nonstick saucepan, the crust bottom (Tah-dig) will come out whole. In a small skillet, heat 1 tablespoon butter, add the barberries and ½ teaspoon of saffron solution and sugar. Stir. Turn off heat. Once sugar melts remove from heat. Place rice on an artist plate. Place a piece of chicken from the basic chicken recipe in the center of the plate. Sprinkle with a dash of cinnamon and 1 spoonful of sauté barberries. Garnish with pistachios and orange rind. Serve with a side of Shirazi salad and lemon dressing.

Be delicious!

Rice with Lima Beans and Dill Palette (Bagala Polo)

2 cups long grain white or brown Basmati rice

1 cup dried dill

2 cups fresh fava beans (if unavailable use one small, frozen package of lima beans and defrost before using)

1 teaspoon cinnamon

1 tablespoon sea salt

4 cups water

4 tablespoons grape seed oil

2 tablespoons butter (optional)

1 tablespoon saffron solution (see Cooking Tips & Notes)

If using beef saucepan roast, include ingredients for Basic Saucepan Roast

Wash and drain the rice. Put the water and salt in a medium saucepan, and bring to a boil. Add rice, and stir once. Reduce the heat to medium-high so the saucepan does not boil over. After 5 minutes, the rice becomes longer in length and starts swimming in the simmering water. Add lima beans, dill and cinnamon and stir gently. Simmer for another 2 minutes. Before the rice gets sticky, drain the water by emptying the saucepan over a colander. Wash the saucepan and dry. Grease the bottom of the saucepan with a butter and oil. Return the rice back to the saucepan. Melt butter and add the saffron solution to it. Pour in a circular form in the center of the rice and spread it by gently fluffing the rice around the solution. Pour the rest of the oil all over the rice. Place a clean towel over the saucepan and firmly press the lid onto the saucepan, securing the towel. Steam for 20 minutes for white rice and 30 minutes for brown rice. Turn over on a platter. Place rice on an artist plate. Place a piece of roasted beef in the center of the plate. Sprinkle with a dash of cinnamon. Serve with a Yogurt and Cucumber salad.

Note: Lima beans may be replaced with 1 cup peeled and ½-inch diced red potatoes. This is called Sheevid Polo instead.

Be delicious!

Rice with Green Beans and Tomato Rice Palette (Lubia Polo)

2 cups long grain white or brown Basmati rice

2 cups fresh green beans, chopped in ½-inch pieces, or 1 small, frozen package (defrost before using)

1 medium onion diced

1 pound ground beef

1 cup tomato juice

fresh juice of one lemon

1 teaspoon turmeric

2 teaspoons cinnamon

1 tablespoon sea salt

4 cups water

5 tablespoons grape seed oil

2 tablespoons butter (optional)

1 teaspoon saffron solution (see Cooking Tips & Notes)

In a medium skillet, brown onion in 1 tablespoon oil over high heat. Add turmeric and stir. Add meat, and brown with onion. In a separate skillet, sauté beans with a dash of salt until the beans shrink in size and glisten. Combine meat and beans in one skillet. Add tomato sauce, lemon juice and 1 teaspoon cinnamon. Season to taste. Reduce to low heat and simmer very slowly for 15 minutes. Wash and drain the rice. Put the water and salt in a medium pot, and bring to a boil. Add rice. Stir once. Reduce the heat to medium-high so the pot does not boil over. After 5 minutes the rice becomes longer in length and starts swimming in the simmering water. Before the rice gets sticky, drain the water by emptying the pot over a colander. Wash the pot and dry. Grease the bottom of the pot with butter and oil. Place a piece of flat bread on the bottom of the pot (optional). Return the rice to the saucepan layering over the flat bread one layer at the time. Between each layer, spread one layer of the meat and green bean mixture. Dash a bit of cinnamon on top. Melt a little butter and add the saffron solution to it. Pour in a circular form in the center of the rice and spread it by gently fluffing the rice around the solution. Pour the rest of the oil all over the rice. Place a clean towel over the pot and firmly press the lid onto the pot, securing the towel. Steam for 20 minutes for white rice and 30 minutes for brown rice. Turn over on a serving platter. If you use a nonstick saucepan, then the crust bottom (Tah-dig) will come out whole. Tah-dig goes great with the sauces of the recipes yet to come. Place rice on an artist plate and serve with a Yogurt and Cucumber Shirazi Salad.

Be delicious!

Rice with Carrots and Raisins Palette (Havij Polo)

2 cups long grain white or brown Basmati rice

1 cup shredded carrots

1 cup raisins

½ cup diced onion

2 teaspoons cinnamon

1 tablespoon sea salt

4 cups water

5 tablespoons grape seed oil or any other flavorless cooking oil

3 tablespoons butter (optional)

2 teaspoons saffron solution (see Cooking Tips & Notes)

ingredients for the Basic Chicken if serving with chicken

In a medium skillet, sauté carrots in a tablespoon of oil and a tablespoon of butter, add a dash of salt and cinnamon. Stir and set aside. Wash and drain the rice. Put the water and salt in a medium saucepan, and bring to a boil. Add rice. Stir once. Reduce the heat to medium-high so the saucepan does not boil over. After 5 minutes the rice becomes longer in length and starts swimming in the simmering water. Before the rice gets sticky, drain the water by emptying the saucepan over a colander. Wash and dry the saucepan. Grease the bottom of the saucepan with butter and oil. Put a layer of rice back to the saucepan, then a layer of carrot and a dash of cinnamon all over it. Continue the layering until no more rice and carrot are left. Melt a little butter and add half of the saffron solution to it. Pour in a circular form in the center of the rice and spread it by gently fluffing the rice around the solution. Pour the rest of the oil all over the rice. Place a clean towel over the saucepan and firmly press the lid onto the saucepan, securing the towel. Steam for 20 minutes for white rice and 30 minutes for brown rice. In a skillet, brown onion with a 1 tablespoon of butter and 1 tablespoon of oil. Add raisins and 1 teaspoon saffron solution. Turn the rice over onto a serving platter and fluff out the rice. Serve on an artist plate with a piece of chicken, a dash of cinnamon and yogurt.

Be delicious!

Saffron Rice with Spinach, Caramelized Onion and Prune Palette (Esfenaj Polo)

- 2 cups long grain white or brown Basmati rice
- 2 cups baby spinach leaves
- ½ cup diced onion
- ½ cup prunes cut in small pieces
- 2 teaspoons cinnamon
- 1 tablespoon sea salt
- 4 cups water
- 5 tablespoons grape seed oil or any other flavorless cooking oil
- 3 tablespoons butter (optional)
- 2 teaspoons saffron solution (see Cooking Tips & Notes)
- ingredients for Basic Saucepan Roast if serving beef

In a medium skillet, sauté half of the onion in one tablespoon oil. Add spinach and a dash of salt. Once spinach wilts, set aside. In the same skillet, brown the rest of onion with 1 teaspoon of butter and 1 tablespoon of oil. Add prunes and 1 teaspoon saffron solution. Wash and drain the rice. Put the water and salt in a medium saucepan. Bring to a boil. Add rice. Stir once. Reduce the heat to medium-high so the saucepan does not boil over. After 5 minutes the rice becomes longer in length and starts swimming in the simmering water. Before the rice gets sticky, drain the water by emptying the saucepan over a colander. Wash and dry the saucepan. Grease the bottom of the saucepan with a little butter. And add a little oil to it. Put a layer of rice back to the saucepan and then a layer of spinach, prune and a dash of cinnamon all over it. Continue the layering until no more rice and spinach mix is left. Melt a little butter and add half of the saffron solution to it. Pour in a circular form in the center of the rice and spread it by gently fluffing the rice around the solution. Pour the rest of the oil all over the rice. Place a clean towel over the saucepan and firmly press the lid onto the saucepan, securing the towel. Steam for 20 minutes for white rice and 30 minutes for brown rice. Turn the rice over onto a serving platter and fluff out the rice. Serve on an artist plate with a piece of saucepan roast beef, a dash of cinnamon and yogurt.

Be delicious!

Rice and Sour Cherries Palette (Albaloo Polo)

2 cups long grain white or brown Basmati rice
3 cups of fresh sour cherries pitted with juice, or 2 cups of sour cherry preserve (if using fresh cherries also ½ cup water and ½ cup sugar in the raw)
2 teaspoons cinnamon
1 tablespoon sea salt
4 cups water
5 tablespoons grape seed oil or any other flavorless cooking oil
3 tablespoons butter (optional)
2 teaspoons saffron solution (see Cooking Tips & Notes)
ingredients for the Basic Chicken

If using fresh sour cherries, place cherries in a small saucepan with sugar and ½ cup water. Bring to a boil, and then reduce heat to medium. Simmer for 30 minutes. Wash and drain the rice. Put the water and salt in a medium pot. Bring to a boil. Add rice. Stir once. Reduce the heat to medium-high so the saucepan does not boil over. After 5 minutes the rice becomes longer in length and starts swimming in the simmering water.

Before the rice gets sticky, drain the water by emptying the saucepan over a colander. Wash and dry the saucepan. Grease the bottom of the saucepan with a little butter, and add a little oil to it. Put a layer of rice back to the saucepan and then a layer of cherries, its syrup and a dash of cinnamon all over it. Continue the layering until no more cherries and syrup is left. Melt a little butter and add half of the saffron solution to it. Pour in a circular form in the center of the rice and spread it by gently fluffing the rice around the solution. Pour the rest of the oil all over the rice. Place a clean towel over the pot and firmly press the lid onto the pot, securing the towel. Steam for 20 minutes for white rice and 30 minutes for brown rice. Turn rice over on a serving platter and fluff out the rice.

Serve on an artist plate with a piece of basic chicken, a dash of cinnamon and some yogurt.

Be delicious!

Rice with Meatballs and Cabbage Palette (Kalam Polo)

2 cups long grain white or brown Basmati rice
½ medium cabbage washed and cut into 1-inch strips
1 medium onion diced
1 pound ground beef
1 cup tomato juice
fresh juice of one lemon
2 teaspoon turmeric

2 teaspoons cinnamon
1 tablespoon sea salt
4 cups water
5 tablespoons grape seed oil
2 tablespoons butter (optional)
1 teaspoons saffron solution (see Cooking Tips & Notes)
ingredients for the Basic Saucepan Roast

Brown the cut cabbage in 2 tablespoons oil, add a dash of salt and set aside. In a bowl, thoroughly mix ground beef with 1 teaspoon cinnamon, 1 teaspoon turmeric, ½ teaspoon salt and ½ teaspoon pepper. Shape small ½-inch meatballs from the mixed ground beef. In a medium skillet, brown onion and meatballs together. Add tomato juice, lemon juice, cinnamon and the rest of turmeric. Season to taste. Reduce to low heat and simmer very slowly for 15 minutes. Wash and drain the rice. Put the water and salt in a medium saucepan, and bring to a boil. Add rice and stir once. Reduce the heat to medium-high so the saucepan does not boil over. After 5 minutes the rice becomes longer in length and starts swimming in the simmering water. Before the rice gets sticky, drain the water by emptying the saucepan over a colander. Wash and dry the saucepan. Grease the bottom of the saucepan with butter and oil. Return the rice back to the saucepan one layer at the time. Between each layer, spread one layer of the meatball and sauce and one layer of cabbage until all the ingredients are inside the saucepan. Dash a bit of cinnamon on top. Melt butter and add the saffron solution to it. Pour in a circular form in the center of the rice and spread it by gently fluffing the rice around the solution. Pour the rest of the oil over the rice. Place a clean towel over the saucepan and firmly press the lid on to the saucepan, securing the towel. Steam for 20 minutes for white rice and 30 minutes for brown rice. Turn over onto a serving platter. Place rice on an artist plate and serve with a Yogurt and Cucumber Shirazi Salad.

Be delicious!

Sweetness

Wish Palette

Rice and Saffron Pudding

1 cup short grain rice

12 cups water

3 cups sugar in the raw

1 teaspoon ground cardamom

¼ cup rose water

3 tablespoons slivered almonds

2 tablespoons pistachios

2 teaspoons cinnamon

3 tablespoons saffron solution (see Cooking notes & Tips)

¼ cup butter

Wash rice. In a bowl, dissolve sugar in two cups of water. Add rose water, cardamom and saffron solution. In a saucepan, put rice and water together and bring to a boil. Reduce heat, and with a large wooden spoon clear the foam around inside the saucepan. Once the saucepan is not boiling over, gently cover and simmer for 45 minutes, stirring occasionally. Add sugar and spice solution. Add butter and half of the almond and simmer for another 25 minutes or until the mix thickens. Transfer to a bowl and decorate with the rest of the almonds, pistachios and cinnamon. Refrigerate to cool before eating. Make a star and wish upon it!

Be delicious!

Receive Palette

Chocolate Raspberry Halva

2 cups sifted all-purpose flour
1 cup melted butter
1½ cups sugar in the raw
1 cup raspberry juice
1 tablespoon rose water
½ teaspoon cinnamon
½ cup cream
1 cup melted, sweet dark chocolate
raspberries and almond livers for garnish

In a small saucepan, melt sugar in raspberry juice and simmer for 15 minutes over low heat. Add rose water and cinnamon, stir and set aside. Mix cream in with melted chocolate. In a large skillet, toast the flour over medium-high heat, stir constantly with a wooden spoon to achieve an even, golden color in the flour. This takes 5 to 10 minutes depending on the speed of stirring. Reduce heat to medium-low. Immediately after the flour is golden, add melted butter stirring constantly for 5 more minutes until the butter and toasted flour are mixed well. Add the raspberry juice solution, stir and mix for 5 more minutes. Add chocolate and cream. Stir and mix. Remove from heat and place in serving bowls. Garnish with almonds and raspberry.

Roses are red, violets are blue.
I like chocolates and diamonds too!

Be delicious!

Celebrate Palette

Rice, Milk and Cardamom Pudding

½ cup short grain rice

2 cups water

3 cups milk

2 tablespoons rose water (optional)

pinch of salt

1 teaspoon ground cardamom

Wash rice, and then put in a saucepan. Add water and pinch of salt and bring to a boil. Reduce heat once it starts to simmer gently and cover the saucepan and cook for 25 minutes. Add milk, cover and cook for 40 more minutes. Add cardamom and rose water and cook for 15 more minutes until it thickens. Transfer to small bowls and refrigerate to cool. Serve with your favorite, fruit, jam, honey, sugar and cinnamon. I like mine with fig jam!

Celebrate the simple things in life.

Be delicious!

Rose Cream Puffs Palette (Naan Khamei)

Pastry

1 cup all-purpose flour

½ cup shortening

1 cup water

4 eggs

1 teaspoon vanilla

¼ teaspoon salt

Filling

1½ cups fresh, heavy cream

1 tablespoon rose water

½ cup sugar

For the pastry: In a medium saucepan, combine shortening [...] gether flour and salt and pour all at once into boiling mixture. Stir vigorously u[...], add vanilla and one egg. Stir vigorously and then add another egg. Repeat addi[...]ll amounts onto a baking sheet. Bake in the center of preheated oven at 725° f[...]

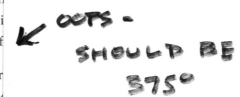

oops – should be 375°

For filling: In a bowl, combine sugar, cream and rose water [...] oss-section and open them, and fill in with cream. You may make a hole in the b[...]g squeeze bottle with the cream. Squeeze the cream from the hole to fill in t[...]

Filling substitutes: You can replace rose water with 2 tables[...]late powder, 1 tablespoon raspberry or strawberry syrup, for various flav[...]

Be delicious!

SWEETNESS • 163

Baklava

Pastry
½ pound each: finely ground raw almonds and ground raw cashews
1½ cups sugar in the raw
2 tablespoons ground cardamom
1 tablespoon rose water

Syrup
1½ cups sugar
¼ cup rose water
1 cup water

Dough
2½ cups sifted all-purpose flour
½ cup melted, unsalted butter
1 tablespoon sugar in the raw
1 egg
¼ cup milk
¼ cup rose water
pistachio slivers for garnish
¼ cup melted butter
¼ cup grape seed oil

For syrup: In a small saucepan, combine sugar and water and bring to a boil to melt the sugar. Once melted, remove from heat. Once it cools, add rose water, stir and set aside.

For filling: Mix all the ground nuts, cardamom and sugar in a food processor until all the ingredients are well grounded.

For dough: In a bowl, mix all the wet ingredients, add flour and mix until the dough is formed and is not sticky to the hands. Grease a half-sheet baking tray by brushing oil on it. Dust an area to roll out dough with a splash of flour. Roll out the dough with a rolling pin to a very thin rectangular piece to fit the baking tray all the way up to its walls. The dough should be about 3mm in thickness. Gently roll the thin dough around the pin and place on the baking tray and roll out over the tray. Evenly, without tearing the dough, spread the filling over the dough. Repeat the step for rolling out another thin layer of dough and lace it over the spread filling. Press dough down evenly to make sure it is in contact with the filling all around. Cut into desired shape, traditionally it is done in diamond shapes by cutting diagonally across the tray using a sharp knife. Do not cut the hanging dough; fold and seal it by pinching the dough together. Bake for 30 minutes or until golden. Remove from oven and pour the syrup over it. Cover and cool for a few hours or over night. Place on an artist plate and garnish with pistachio slivers. Serve with a nice Earl Grey tea.

Dough substitute: You can make this in less time if you use phyllo dough.

Be delicious!

Max's Ginger Bread

1 cup whole wheat flour

3 cups all-purpose flour

1 cup brown sugar

1 cup granulated sugar

1 cup unsalted butter (soft room temperature)

4 fresh eggs

1 cup milk warmed to 110°

1 tablespoon dry yeast

1 teaspoon baking soda

dash of salt

2 tablespoons ground ginger

1 teaspoon cinnamon

1 extra egg, beaten for brushing

pinch of sesame seeds to sprinkle for topping (optional)

In mixing bowl, blend butter, brown and white sugar until creamy. Add eggs, milk and dry yeast. Mix the rest of dry ingredients separately and add to the batter mix until well blended. Cover the dough in a warm place for 45 minutes until the dough rises to almost double. Push the dough down and cut in equal-sized slices and make ball shape portions. Place the balls on a greased baking pan and let stand for half an hour in room temperature. Gently push down each ball and brush with beaten eggs. Bake at 350° for 30 minutes or until golden brown. Let bread cool. Serve on an artist plate with cheese, butter or whatever your heart desires. My mother often baked this delicious bread, but my brother Max made it after she passed away and wrote the recipe.

Be delicious!

Drinks

Angels in Oasis

1 pint white chilled champagne
fresh squeezed juice of 2 limes
½ cup sugar in the raw
1 shot crème de ment
mint for garnish
¼ cup heated water

Melt sugar in heated water, add lime juice. Add crème de ment. Pour champagne in a pitcher. Pour mint and lime mix over it and stir once. Pour in individual glasses, with ice if preferred. Garnish with mint.

Be delicious!

Sin-a-Man Apple Martini

1 shot cinnamon schnapps
1 shot apple liqueur
2 shots vodka
1 shot triple sec
1 wedge lemon
1 cup apple juice
4 crushed cinnamon candy
1 cup crushed ice
cinnamon stick
wedge of red apple

Place the crushed candy on a flat plate. Slightly wet the rim of a martini glass with the lemon wedge and dip into the candy plate so the rim will be covered with cinnamon candy. Put ice in a martini shaker followed by all the liquid ingredients. Shake and mix. Pour the mix in the candy rimmed glass. Garnish with cinnamon stick and apple wedge.

Adam's toast to Eve before biting the apple!

Be delicious!

Bloody Mary Fun Fest

BFF Cocktail

8 cups chilled tomato juice
2 cups vodka of your choice
fresh squeezed juice of 4 limes
¼ cup sugar in the raw
1 teaspoon cinnamon
2 teaspoons Tabasco sauce
¼ pound each of Italian dry salami, roast beef, smoked turkey
cubed sharp cheddar cheese
cubed jalapeño cheese
olives and pickles
4 tall celery stalks
a few small romaine lettuce leaves
a few cherry tomatoes
ice cubes
bread cracker sticks or long pretzels (optional)

Roll up the meats and skew them on toothpicks. Add olives, pickles, cheese and tomato and make various combinations of skewers. Attach two or three lettuce leaves to each celery stalk using the toothpicks. Attach the skewers to the lettuce/celery tree. Mix chilled tomato juice, lime juice, salt, cinnamon and Tabasco sauce in a pitcher. Add ice cubes. Pour into tall glasses. Place a lettuce/celery tree into the glass. Add the bread stick or pretzels.

Be delicious!

There is art at the of darkness

&

There is light at the end of art.

Acknowledgments

Thank you to the following people for their support and guidance.

My angels: Ahmad, Nicole, Ryan and Peeshy.

My muses: Pouran for her art. Azar for her fire. Soussan for her heart. Max for his wisdom.

For their assistance: Robyn Short, Esmeralda Cruz, Kat Smith and Russ Riddle.